Kathy,
This book was written by our retired minister at UU.
Pat

cycles
of
reflection

ON THE MYSTERY
AND CHALLENGE OF LIVING

ROBERT E. SENGHAS

Collected and Edited by Julia V. Blake

Lilac Mountain Books
Jericho, Vermont
2001

ISBN 0-9709845-0-2

Library of Congress Number 2001089543

Printed in the United States of America

Publisher: Lilac Mountain Books
Jericho, Vermont

Editor: Julia V. Blake

Designer: Vicky McCafferty

Calligraphic squiggle: Jean Evans

Cover photograph: www.comstock.com

Printer: Thomson-Shore, Inc.
Dexter, Michigan

Second Printing

We are seekers who wish to discover and to face what is true about our own lives and about the world in which we live. We like to hide from truth when it tells us what we prefer not to hear, but we must continue as pilgrims seeking to know what is real, in its meanness and its glory, and to live as whole persons in the midst of our joys and our sorrows.

We seek a renewal of the inner spirit which can animate our lives, brighten our dark times, and intensify our times of joy. We seek and are sought by that spirit which is within each of us. Remember that to those who seek, it will be given; to those who knock, the door will be opened; and that if we ask, we shall receive.

—Senghas

Nothing else matters much — not wealth, nor learning,
nor even health — without this gift:
the spiritual capacity to keep zest in living.
This is the creed of creeds, the final deposit and distillation
of all our important faiths:
that we should be able to believe in life.

—Harry Emerson Fosdick, adapted
(quoted often by Senghas)

contents

acknowledgements

First I want to thank Bob and Dorrie Senghas for their support of this project and for the time they have spent reviewing the manuscript. I appreciate Bob's generosity in lending the original sermons and meditations to me for an extended period of time and his willingness to let me edit his words. He has been very trusting to allow me to carry out this project, and I hope that the resulting book will honor him and that he will feel his trust was warranted.

Many other people have given generously of their time, knowledge, or financial resources to help make possible this book. Several years ago Howard Taylor, Evelyn Carter, and Stan Miller kindly read the first draft and offered helpful suggestions and encouragement. From time to time Kathleen Ryan and Jean Evans offered guidance on design and procedure. Dian Mueller set me on the trail that led to Vicky McCafferty, and also meticulously did the final proof-reading. My husband, Stephen Gelatt, assisted me greatly with the computer, as well as reading the manuscript and offering suggestions on text and design.

The generous financial support of the following people is tremendously appreciated: an anonymous donor, Gary Kowalski and Dori Jones, the Women's Alliance of the First Unitarian Universalist Society, and especially Susanna Adams, without whose contribution the book could not have been published. In addition, Susanna spent many hours in detailed editing of the text, as well as offering helpful design suggestions, enthusiasm and moral support.

Vicky McCafferty has been a real pleasure to work with, cheerfully steering me through the confusing world of computers and publishers. Without her at the helm these past six months, it is hard to imagine how the book would ever have materialized.

And finally, again, I and all who find wisdom and healing in his words, are grateful to Bob Senghas for sharing his vision with us.

biographical data

Robert Erwin Senghas was born in 1928 and grew up in the Cleveland, Ohio, area. In 1950 he graduated from Yale University with a degree in Economics, followed by a JD degree from Harvard Law School in 1953. Following two years in the U.S. Marine Corps, Bob practiced law for five years in San Francisco. In 1952 he married Dorothy Caiger, a lifelong Unitarian, and they have three grown sons and four grandchildren.

After leaving the practice of law, Bob received a Master of Divinity degree from Starr King School for the Ministry in 1963, and then served seven years as minister of the Unitarian Universalist Church in Davis, California. In 1971 he and Dorrie moved back East, where Bob served as minister of the Wellesley Hills (Mass.) Unitarian Universalist Society until 1974, when he assumed the position of Executive Vice President of the continental Unitarian Universalist Association in Boston. From there, in 1979, Bob moved to the minister's position at the First Unitarian Universalist Society in Burlington, Vermont, serving ten years until his retirement in 1989. In 1984 the Starr King School awarded Bob an honorary doctorate, the S.T.D. (Sacred Theology Doctorate.)

Since 1982 Bob has been a student of John Daido Loori Roshi, Abbot of the Zen Mountain Monastery in New York, where Bob is currently a senior student. Bob is past President and a current member of the Board of the continental Unitarian Universalist Buddhist Fellowship, as well as one of the founders of the Zen Affiliate of Vermont.

Bob and Dorrie live in Burlington still, where Bob has been on the boards of various organizations (such as Planned Parenthood of Northern New England, the Vermont Mozart Festival, and the Committee on Temporary Shelter,) as well as learning to play the viola, sailing, and serving as the New Hampshire-Vermont UU District representative on the Board of the continental Unitarian Universalist Association.

foreword

Light and Shadow, Ebb and Flow: Cycles of Reflection

I begin with an expression of my gratitude to Bob Senghas, a gratitude with which I feel I am speaking for many other persons as well. We feel fortunate to have been graced by Bob's presence and his wise words while serving as minister in Burlington where many lives were touched and strengthened. My own beliefs and attitudes toward life's challenges have been profoundly affected by his vision of reality. This continues as an ongoing process, for I am still learning from his words and trying to increasingly incorporate into my daily life the truths he revealed.

As I reviewed, selected, and organized the meditations and sermons, I was struck by what a consistent body of thought these words represent. It is true, I suppose, that every good minister offers listeners a coherent world-view, a particular vision of life, and the reader will recognize the major themes of Bob's vision as they recur in various topics he addresses.

Over the span of ten years as minister in Burlington Bob looked deeply at the questions, *What is life? What is reality?* and *How best can we respond to what we see as life, or reality?* Always he urged his listeners to consider these questions deeply and then to decide, commit, and act, based on our own beliefs.

Like an Old Testament prophet or a modern day counselor, Bob constantly and passionately challenged, encouraged, admonished, clarified, comforted. Unblinking in the face of mystery or darkness, he thought very seriously about life's experiences and reported honestly what he saw and the meaning he made of it. He always suggested choices for attitudes and for action, and urged his listeners to consider deeply the seriousness of those choices and actions.

I have an image of Bob, the sermon-giver, as the conductor of an orchestra, leading us—the fellow musicians—to address various music, sometimes exuberant, sometimes mournful, sometimes questioning, sometimes affirming, but always with depth and passion. Like any good conductor, he had tremendous respect for the power of the music and the musicians.

His vision of reality is one of light and shadows, cycles of birth and death, all within a Great Mystery or Oneness larger than any individual, yet in which each person participates. (Those familiar with Buddhism will recognize Bob's affinity with the Buddhist perspective.) His overall statement is a passionate belief in the value of life, the power that can be expressed by human beings, the awesomeness of the mystery in which we partake. Always evident is some sense that there is no separation between self and other or the larger universe; we are all part of One.

It is as if Bob Senghas holds a marvelous piece of many-sided Vermont marble in his hands, turning it slowly so that the light falls at different angles on its face, always presenting a new perspective, sometimes allowing us to feel we are seeing into the innerness of the stone, sometimes reflecting back only light or shadow.

The choice as to which meditations and sermons to include in this collection has been a highly personal one—I chose those that spoke most powerfully to me, and I realize that some other individual would most certainly have chosen differently. I offer this collection as words to ponder carefully and deliberately, at a pace slow enough to allow them to reverberate and simmer within you. The reader may find it best to use these readings as meditative pieces, picking and choosing, reading one at a time and reflecting upon it.

The ebb and flow of life, the cycles of the soul's seasons, penetrate Bob's vision and call forth recurring symbols of death, rebirth, darkness, light, and the seasons of the year. At first I attempted to organize the selections into clear seasonal categories, but the beauty and wisdom of these words is such that they resist any easy categorization, so I gave that up. The organization and headings that I finally chose are very rough, and merely an attempt to give the reader some cursory guidance. The headings are mostly titles of sermons or quotes from the excerpts.

A few times I have left whole sermons almost intact, as I felt that omitting sections would detract from the power or the poetry of the selection, but usually I have included only parts of sermons. Many of the short selections are "meditations"—words he spoke at the end of an extended period of silent meditation each Sunday. One or two excerpts are from sermons given somewhere other than Burlington or in a year before or after 1979-89, and these are indicated in the Notes at the end, as are dates for all the selections. With Bob's permission, I have omitted the ellipses (indicating the deletion of phrases, words, or sentences), in order to avoid interrupting the flow of thought or meaning and only when Bob's original meaning was not altered in any way.

This has been a highly satisfying work for me, and I am grateful for having had the opportunity to immerse myself in it. My hope is that it will give soul sustenance to some others as it has so richly to me.

Julia V. Blake,
member of the First Unitarian Universalist
Society of Burlington, Vermont.
February 2001

cycles of reflection

sunrise is real: rebirth and renewal

Remember the spring which lies within each of us, waiting to be born, even as we lie in a winter of the soul.

～

The old year is dead, and its pages of life are no longer open. Its record of moments, hours, and days of joys and sorrows is closed. Now we enter a new time, with a book that opens a new page to us each morning. May we face each new day with gratitude that we have been given not only the gift of life, but the gift of knowing that we have that gift. Let us greet each new day with a *yes* to the greater life of the universe in which we have our little parts to play. May we resolve to be worthy of the gift of life we have received.

～

We do not understand how the gift of life and of the spirit comes to us in our darkness. But it does come to us, over and over again, as it has come for thousands of years—if we have faith that it will come and if we open ourselves up to receive it. Our power to respond can be reborn, creativity once lost can be recaptured, and the capacity to love and to be loved can be revived.

The Messiah is born when we bring ourselves to birth. Somewhere within each of us a messiah waits—it is that part of us which will bring us new hope and new life. Look for the messiah within you! Bring that messiah to birth!

~

The seasons spin, and we remember the years which began in hope and expectation, years which were fulfilled in both joy and disappointment. May we search with the fullness of our wills for the faith that lies in the heart of each one of us, the faith that sends us forth into the unknown future to be bearers of light and hope and comfort. So may we be co-creators of life, worthy of the spirit which brought us into being, transmitters of that spirit to others now and to come.

~

We stand in amazement at the glories, the vastness, and the intricacy of the worlds beyond this little planet and at the world within our own bodies. May our hearts and minds be open to feel the unity beyond the diversity of those worlds; let us live out our years with the freshening experience of each day's dawn and its promise of a new day. May we have eyes to see, ears to hear, and hearts to feel the mystery that is around us and within us, that we may, in our fleeting lives, love what is eternal.

~

There are seasons in our souls: times of withering, times of coldness, times of renewal, times of sun and light. May the force which drives nature to its fulfillment be brought forth in us too. Within each of us is the power to love and to care, which waits only for our wills and our own acts to bring it forth. Let us be instruments of that power which (as it does in all of nature) comes through us but not from us, the power which waits only for us to bring it forth.

~

In the midst of the busyness and the distractions of our daily lives we are often heedless of the passing moments when life offers itself to us. May we pause to widen our awareness of the things we take for granted, the sacred in the ordinary.

May the morning of each new day be greeted as the unfolding of a mystery and a beauty that has never been revealed before and will never be revealed again. We know that each of us is part of what we contemplate, one wholeness, one beauty, one eternity.

~

Each of us in this life can be resurrected or, if you will, renewed, revived, renovated, or filled with resurgence. The process to health is to go through a grief process in which we accept the death of the old self of hope and of fantasy. There is no resurrection in this life without grief for what has died in us, but if we are willing to go through that grief, there is the possibility for us, in this life, to be revived again and again.

We are reminded by the resurrection of nature that we can look at the dying shell of our own old life, with its broken dreams and lost illusions of success and perpetual health; we can let go of that old self, let it drop away. We can find new hope and new life and freedom in a more real, mortal, limited, and divine incarnation in this our own body and mind.

~

May we venture forth into a new season, open to the ebb and flow about us. May we accept the invitation to dance which life offers us, and realize our true natures.

～

Our spirits grow dull by the repetition of familiar faces and events. In our lives of habit we yearn for a glorious breaking forth of light. We wish to be stirred by a passionate response to beauty, by an electrifying act of justice, by a stirring vision of truth. Instead, may we seek so to live in our world of the commonplace that we become bearers, rather than spectators, of beauty and justice and truth. Let us not seek ecstasy, but rather seek to be fully present to one another and to the world we face every day.

～

On a day of warmth and sunshine we remember the long dark days of winter. On a day of returning life in the earth we remember the times we have known when we too have felt the revival of life within ourselves after a winter of despair and self-doubt. May we turn to use the gifts outside us and within us, through which we can be restored and reconciled to live again in a world that waits for our restoration and our reconciliation.

～

The spirit which animates our lives is found and lost again and again within us. Our lives have been quickened by its presence and darkened by its absence. We rejoice for those times when we have felt its presence, and in our hours of weakness and despair, our search for the renewal of that spirit prepares us to receive it, when it wells up again within us.

Let us shun false and easy words of solace and know that the spirit of life and wholeness comes to us not when we dwell upon our failures, but when we recognize them and resolve to do better. Let us keep the faith that the spirit of wholeness will come again to us when we are true to our deepest selves.

~

Are you ready, are you willing, are you able to accept the rebirth of hope? Are you ready for a rebirth of new life in *you?* We who are no longer children are being asked if we are ready to seek and to find new life within ourselves.

The freshness and newness of childhood can be born in each of us, in us who are jaded, sated, self-absorbed, darkened, and depressed. We must wait like one who waits in the womb to be born. We must not wait in expectation of an ecstasy of religious experience; rather, we must wait for the simple unfolding of ourselves in life, for the simple becoming of who we can be. Out of our darkness there will be light and new life again. We are born and die and are reborn many times during our lives.

~

We turn a new leaf in our book of life to face the open pages of the coming days. In our backward glance we see the pilgrims who have passed this way before us: not only the renowned heroes and founders, the Moses, the Buddha, the Jesus, the Mohammed, but the millions of women and men who have passed without trace today, the millions who have faced each new year with grace and inspiration.

May we be open to life as they were open, facing the open pages of today and tomorrow with gratitude for the gift of life, with gratitude that we are the animal that is conscious of its own life in its beginnings and its endings. Let us live in love of the greater life of which we are part and show our love in what we do for that great web of existence. May our word to the open page, and whatever may come to fill it, be *yes*.

～

Life itself is a crucifixion and a resurrection, and we go through that cycle many times while we are still alive. There is a resurrection that waits for each of us, within ourselves.

～

the fundamental experience: the life of the spirit

The religious experience, the fundamental experience, which can occur to us in our everyday lives as well as in special times and places, is the experience of an intense and profound feeling of *being at home in the world.* Those are the special times when we look about us, as Abraham Maslow said, with "wonder, awe, reverence, humility, surrender, and worship," when we lose our concern for our little egos in the face of this vast universe and within the walls of the very room which is our home.

It is possible to find a new faith. Faith means trust: a trust in life, in the value of life, a trust that our being alive here and now matters, a trust that what we do or do not do matters. Whether our new faith or trust is traditional or nontraditional, theistic or non-theistic, with a congregation or solitary, when we have such a faith it means that our lives are grounded in something we believe, something to which we commit ourselves. We today are fully as capable of a life of faith as were our ancestors. The life of the spirit awaits us, if we open our hearts to that spirit.

⌣

At the heart of religion is the fundamental emotional experience of trust—a trust, despite the terrible injustices and inequities in the world, despite the impersonality of the forces of nature and the cruelties of nature and human beings, that in some way we can commit ourselves emotionally to the life of the universe; we pour ourselves into it as we live and even as we die.

As a major alternative to stoic resignation, it is possible to live in trust: that our life is worth living and a trust in ourselves, that we can be instruments of caring. The trust of stoicism is a trust that the universe operates by orderly principles, but the trust of religion is beyond that. Stoicism has us walk through the valleys of our troubles by acceptance, resignation, and perseverance, while the trust of faith leads us out into the unknown with a simple commitment of the self.

I do not mean some kind of irrational trust in violation of common sense or the realities of the world, nor do I mean trust in some supernatural intervention from some divine source. I mean only that we can face each new day and take each new step with an open heart and spirit.

There is another option: to look upon life as a struggle which must be fought to our last breath. This option views life as a fight of humanity against the stars, a fight which we are doomed to lose, but which we must wage nevertheless. I believe it expresses one of the worst ways possible to face life and death. If there is a Hell on earth, it is to burn with rage day after day against whatever life has brought us and especially against the knowledge of our mortality. Anger is normal for us to feel at times, in our disappointments and frustrations and in our last illness, but if we have not been able to replace that anger with the acceptance of the stoic or the trust of faith, then we become snarling animals at bay against the hunter.

These, then, are three of the choices which we have: a fight to the death, the acceptance of stoicism, or the life of trust. Choose, and live.

❧

Religion is not what we profess on Sunday morning, but what we say and do on Monday in home and work. Our religion is our speaking and our action: for truth against evasion and deception, for justice against the injustices of our daily lives and of our national power, and for compassion instead of the hardened heart, the averted eye, and the deafened ear.

❧

The tendency to intellectualize so much about religious experience that we lose that experience itself has been a curse. We should, of course, be using our intellects in order to understand our religion, but the danger is that we will get so wrapped up in the ideas of religion that we get away from the source of religion in our own personal experience.

❧

The lilacs are beginning to open their leaves. All the knowledge that botany will ever bring us can never explain the emotion we may feel when we see those leaves open, for beneath and behind that process we detect a reality and a power that we can never know directly. We behold the *mystery* through the opening of those lilacs.

When we see the birth and growth of a child, when we observe its opening up to the world as it accepts love and begins to return that love to others, we behold evidence of a mystery. All that we know or ever will know of genetics and environmental conditioning will not diminish that mystery; indeed, the more we know, the greater evidence we have of the mystery which produces all life.

The love and compassion we give and receive from one another have a source which must be a mystery. All the discoveries of psychology—all our knowledge of sexuality and sociology—describe only the effects of that mystery. Our ability to see the structure and relationships in our physical and human world is itself another manifestation of the same power that opens the leaves of the lilac.

The beginning, the flowering, and the ending of each life— these are mysteries which reveal themselves to us if we stand before them. The experience of those mysteries is not that of a soft, squishy piety. It is awesome. It can come to us in the gentleness of the opening of the lilacs, or in the terrors of disease and destruction. However it comes to us or we to it, the experience of mystery is not only the dower of true science, as Einstein said, but also the dower of all true religion.

This brings me to the word *God.* There are those who would say simply that God is the same as the mystery, that the mystery is what God is. But my own belief is that there is a distinction between the mystery and something at the heart of the Jewish and Christian traditions which has had the name of God. This tradition tells us that God is the power which has brought that mystery into being and the power which creates all that is. We are created by that power; the mystery is created by that power; and our capacity to comprehend that mystery in some dim way comes from the all-inclusive power we have named *God.*

I accept the word *God* as a name for that ultimate power reluctantly, but I accept it because I believe that power needs a name in order for us to think about it and to help us realize we stand before it, that we live in it, move in it, and have our being in it.

Next we come to the word *prayer.* Prayer is our opening ourselves up to the mystery of existence and our willingness to stand before the ultimate power that is revealed in everything we see and know. Often called meditation, prayer is what we do when we focus our selves to stand in the midst of our daily world and look at the manifestations—the revelations—of the mystery of life and of the universe, when we have intimations of the power beneath and within all that is or can be. Prayer is an experience of the emotions, and it can take various forms.

Prayer can be in the form of our contemplation of the mystery and the power, as we look at the lilac unfolding or regard the face of a child or the compassionate love of one human being for another. Prayer can be the experience we may have when we realize that we ourselves are instruments of power, and that as we act, the source of our power is acting through us (for good or for ill.) Prayer can be in the form of our experience of thanksgiving—a thanksgiving not that the world is as we would have it be, but simply that the world is as it is.

Prayer can be the experience we have when we address the highest and deepest within us on those occasions when we must make a decision of the will to pursue the good or the caring way in some specific situation. Prayer is not then to a God *out there,* but to the divine element within each of us, to summon within ourselves power to exercise our own will.

Finally, prayer can be the experience of the ultimate acceptance—the acceptance of the truth that the ways of the Creator, of the power of being itself, are not our ways: "not my will, but thine." In the words of the prayer of Jesus, "Thy will be done." Prayer does not ask for anything; it opens us to receive—everything.

It does not matter whether any of us use the words *mystery, God,* or *prayer.* What does matter is that in our lives—in our daily, mundane lives—there are times when we are willing to be open to the mystery, willing to stand before the power and feel its awesome strength, willing to be open to the life of life. Before that mystery and that power, we give thanks, we praise, and we say yes.

Religious life means a life which is lived with a consciousness of the presence of something ultimate in it. A person can have this religious element without a belief in a God of the Jewish or Christian tradition, and he or she may not want to use the God-vocabulary at all. Many who are regular church-attendees, and who find the God-vocabulary quite comfortable, are a long way from a religious life; they live without any sense of the ultimate, without any quality of the religious. For many, God is about as awesome as the sofa in their living room, part of the friendly furniture of life.

The religious is not a doctrine, nor is it a statement of belief. The religious is the power or the source out of which we and all of Creation are sprung. The experience of the religious is the experience of that power.

The heart of religion is the personal experience; the foundation of religion is in the religious experience of each individual. Like no other experience, this is one in which we sense that we are part of something infinite and eternal, which includes us and all that is, all that ever has been, all that ever will be, here and everywhere. That infinite and eternal whole—which is accessible to the experience of each of us—is called "God" and given particular descriptions and stories in the Jewish, Christian, and other traditions, but it is not necessary that we call it God, or even that we give it any name at all.

To be religious means to have an experience of the infinite and the eternal, which gives life a quality otherwise missing. It makes the thought of death acceptable and the process of dying more bearable, whether or not there is a belief in life after death.

The religious experience of something ultimate and infinite within and beyond our personal selves gives us the ability to perceive the presence of that ultimate, infinite quality in other beings and other things. That experience is the root of our faith in the value of life and love and morality, a faith which cannot be proven in the way of objective proof, but which makes it possible for us to live in trust and to endure the absence of life, love, and goodness in our encounters with death, uncaring, and evil.

The pathways of religion are the way of the mind (which is knowledge), the way of the heart (which is devotion or love), the way of the hands, (which is good works), and the way of intuition (which is meditation).

If a religion is to be alive and real, it must stand on the boundary of society and call our social and political systems to account. A religion that does not give its adherents a sense that there is some ultimate value for their lives is a failed religion. A religion which also does not make us uncomfortable with the world is also a failed religion. A real religion at times must make us uncomfortable, and then show us how we can transform ourselves by what we do about that discomfort.

Happiness is not something anyone can give anyone else; each of us must come to understand what happiness can be in this life, and how to attain and live happiness, in spite of everything. Happiness must be won.

We each must learn to develop our own way of belief, so that we can accept and face a world that will continue to be inhumane and destructive in many respects. One of our religious tasks is to understand how to accept that truth itself is impartial and that the facts are not necessarily friendly. Truth may tell us the limitations of our life and the narrowness or breadth of our options. It may tell us of our health or sickness, our mortality, our strengths and our weaknesses. Our task is to learn how to live in that truth, how to live in the real world.

The problem is not the resolution of some conflict between science and religion, for there is no necessity of such a conflict, if we can accept whatever truth has to tell us, welcome or unwelcome. The problem, rather, is what we do after we have seen the truth. Are we willing to accept and live in a world that is largely beyond our control? Are we willing to pursue the winning of a happy life, in spite of all the grief, suffering, and defeat that each of us will encounter?

In short, are we willing to live a real life? That is a question that science cannot answer, for the answer lies within the mind and the will of each of us. That is the question addressed by every religion worthy of the modern age, whether that religion is liberal or conservative, Christian or non-Christian. Are we willing to live a real life?

It is the task of a lifetime, the task of maturity, for each of us to work out our personal answer to that question. It is a work that must encounter discouragement and despair and still press on, a work that continues all of our lives. That work is the way of religion.

Religion is a matter of the heart, not the intellect. To be religious means to make some kind of affirmation of our total being, rather than to affirm some philosophical or scientific principle with our intellect.

If we as individuals make our ultimate concern keeping our lives in touch with the ground of being, if we are most concerned that in our lives we have an experience of that infinite power of being out of which everything comes, then we live authentic religious lives, lives of true religious experience. On the other hand, as Paul Tillich said, if we substitute some lesser concern—such as money or success—in place of a concern for the real ground of being, then we have made that lesser concern our personal ultimate concern; in such a case, we have become idolatrous. If success is our religion, then we have come to worship the idol of success. If pleasure becomes our ultimate concern, then our experience of pleasure becomes an idolatrous religious experience.

Religious experience may be authentic or idolatrous, and the opposite of religious experience is indifference to any ultimate concern. The issue is whether in our own lives we are living idolatrously or making our ultimate concern that which is truly ultimate. The critical issue is the quality of our lives, the experience of the religious, and not the words we use.

—

The only security is the security that accepts the presence of doubt. The great questions of our lives must be answered with responses that include doubt and uncertainty. The great decisions of our lives must be made with the awareness that there is great doubt as to the full consequences of those decisions. Who can venture on the great voyage into a lifetime commitment to another or into parenthood without great faith, a faith which takes doubt and uncertainty into itself? Who can look at the world and the time in which we live and then act without faith, a faith which takes into itself anxieties and doubts that goodness and justice will prevail?

Who has truly prevailed who does not understand what it means to say, "My God, my God, why have you forsaken me?" Who is there who can say a profound *yes* to life, without having heard first the murmur of doubt and despair? Who can find the power to face disease, the loss of loved ones, old age, and death, without first knowing the darkness of doubt and despair?

The real questions of life and death will never be answered for us. If any answer is to come to each of us, it will have to come *from* each of us, for ourselves. No one else—no creed, no clergy, no leader—can tell us what we must do to be capable of meeting the challenges of life.

We are called to a faith, a trust beyond any chance of proof, that this moment is real, that our lives are real, that what we say and leave unsaid matters, that what we do and leave undone matters, that life is as real as death is real. We have been given this beautiful, ugly, glorious, terrible, joyful, and painful world as our home for a few years, and in those years and in each moment we are called by a power greater than ourselves to be who we are and to do what must be done. I cannot give you that faith, but it is yours to take.

~

Religion is not only what we believe, but what we do; not only what we value most deeply, but how we act to bring our values into the world; not only our sense of the oneness of all that is, but how we act to heal and to harmonize what is broken and ill and out of harmony.

May we have the courage of our faith to challenge what is evil and wrong in ourselves and in our relations with others; may we have the courage to perform the painful acts that are necessary on the road to healing and reconciliation and peace.

~

There is great value in looking upon aspects of our lives in terms of calls to heroism, as in the times we face surgery, or dangerous or painful episodes, or calls for sacrificial love. However, when I think of the value of life itself or the value of my own life, I have found that the model of life as a heroic struggle is inadequate: my trying to be a hero does not sustain me religiously or spiritually.

The Tibetan Buddhist teacher, Chögyam Trungpa, coined the term *spiritual materialism,* which describes much of what passes for religion. One who seeks to have her or his name placed in the cosmic yearbook in the sky with many inches of biography attesting to one's generosity, or love, or good works, is a spiritual materialist, as is the one who seeks to be worthy of an epitaph which reads, "Here lies a fully self-realized humanist."

Each of us is called to heroism from time to time, but if we make the hero our model, we become susceptible to spiritual materialism. The seeking of salvation, the desire to have something beyond our own death, the hope for eternal life, the expectation of a restoration of lost ties in a world to come, the hope to be fully self-realized, these are all forms of spiritual materialism.

What is needed is not a religion for some future time, but a religion for each present moment. What we need is not a religion for *something*, but a religion for *no thing*, a religion for nothing. We have all the Heaven and Hell there is in this very moment, and in the next moment, and the moment after that. As Jesus said, "Do not be anxious about tomorrow, for tomorrow will be anxious for itself. Let each day's trouble be sufficient for the day."

When we look at ourselves and at the world around us in this present moment, we are being summoned to acts of caring. We do not need the carrot of Heaven nor the stick of the fear of Hell to make us do what needs to be done. We do not need the hope of achieving some image of complete self-realization nor the fear of personal failure to make our lives worthy ones. We do not need spiritual materialism to cloud our clear look at ourselves and our world of good and evil. This is it! This is ours to love at this moment, with all its good and its evil!

◆

The way of religion is the way of living on the boundary of society. To be religious demands that we have values deeper than social convention. Those who live in strict conformity with the demands of our culture and society must take their values from outside themselves: they look to others to tell them what is right, or just, or true. A religious person may appear to be conventional in the ordinary course of social life, but has a moral and spiritual compass that lies within himself or herself.

◆

It is important that we have some sense of ultimacy, some sense that what we do or do not do matters, that we have a faith, a trust, to put ourselves into life, to stake our lives and the limited time of our living upon certain values. It is important to us to celebrate life and the ultimate quality of life in all its transiency.

As Forrest Church has noted, the double knowledge—that we know that we are alive and that we are going to die—is the source of all religion. That does not mean that religion is only about living and dying, but that as we struggle to understand that knowledge, to live in the presence of that knowledge, and to act with that knowledge, there is a quality or depth that can come into our lives which is religious.

⊱

Religion is the way each of us comes to terms with our own life, the way we each find an ultimate security in living in the face of the certainties and uncertainties of life and death, success and failure, joy and pain, self–fulfillment and self–betrayal. Religion is the way we come to realize that we are at home in a world that is beautiful and ugly, benign and indifferent. Religion does not shield us from grief or pain, but it makes that grief and pain bearable. It does not shield us from the real world, but it allows us to live and to affirm our living in the real world of beauty and ugliness, joy and indifference, death and birth.

⊱

Beyond a certain point we are unable to affirm life and to love, unless we have developed a faith in life, a faith which is an act of commitment by our whole selves, an act of affirmation, a *yes* to the world. That faith is essentially a religious commitment, although it may not be traditional or theistic or embodied in any institutional religion. It is an act of the will, and no one can do it for us. I have known people raised in the most privileged families who have been unable to live by faith, and I have known many who grew up with emotional, physical, and economic handicaps who have that faith. Neither I nor anyone else can give you your faith; only you can give it to yourself.

In the New Testament the Greek word for faith is *pistis,* which means both faith and trust, underscoring the point that without faith we are not able to trust life. Indeed, faith *is* trust. Without that trustful commitment, we are not able to love fully or to care fully or to affirm the world fully. We are like a tree on the edge of a cliff that must use all its strength to cling to the side of the rock so as not to fall into the abyss; too much of our energy goes into protecting and insulating ourselves from the realities we dare not face. We deny or avoid as long as we can, until we are forced to surrender to our mortality in stoic despair. There are many who live such lives.

The fulfillment of faith is that we are able to keep trust in life, and so become the loving and caring and open men and women we can be. We shall not escape pain and disappointment and death, but we will realize the power to bear what life brings. And beyond that, we will be able to make our life itself a song of praise and affirmation.

Seek a faith that celebrates life, a faith that offers a thanksgiving for the gift of life and love and the wonder of all that is. But go further and seek a faith that addresses the hard questions of life: the infirmities of age and disease, the injustices, the unreason, the immoralities, the suffering, the ultimate death of all living things.

Too often we live with heads bowed by fear and limited knowledge and awareness of our meager power. Let us have a faith that faces the world as it is, with its cruelty and indifference as well as its benevolence, its unreason as well as its patterns of meaning, its mortalities as well as its vitalities. Have a faith that is worthy of the gift of consciousness we have received: a faith to live in the world before us, a faith which makes us agents of creating a world of greater good, deeper love, and abiding justice.

⌐

The religious truth that sets us free from the bondage of human limitation and death will not come from science nor from anywhere outside ourselves. That is a truth that we must find within ourselves, each of us, a truth that we must embrace with passion despite its uncertainties.

I believe that this world with all its joy and sorrow is a holy place. I believe that every person in this world, every living being, every nonliving being, every rock—all are holy. I believe that every moment of time is holy. I believe that pain and suffering are always bad, and that the intentional infliction of pain can be justified only when we can expect it to prevent greater pain. I believe that beauty is its own justification, that goodness is its own reward, and that the practice of goodness results in a deeper spiritual life. I believe that we came from out of a great mystery, and each of us shall return to a great mystery, and that our task is to make this passage between those mysteries worthy for our having been here.

I believe that we are sustained in this life by something ultimate, and that we are all part of one whole in this real world of beauty and ugliness, goodness and evil. And I believe that my faith and trust—if I make them strong enough—will sustain me through all my days.

You cannot give me your faith, and I cannot give you mine. That is something each of us must do for ourselves, but the message of faith and trust can be passed from one human being to another.

~

The denial of religion begins in the refusal to look. When we look, see, love, and act, we are saying yes to life, which is the affirmation at the heart of every religion worthy of its believers. Those who can follow that pilgrimage to a yes find that their own mortality becomes unimportant. They know that the religious question is not "What will happen to me tomorrow?" but "What calls me today? What lies before me this very moment?"

~

I have faith in the power that resides in each one of us to know the good and to do the good. I have faith that each of us has the gift to see that we are part of one great family of all living things, and that we have the power to heal as well as to hurt. I believe that within us we have the power to meet the fears, the suffering, and the challenges of our lives with courage, resolution, compassion and action. There is a force that moves in us and through us that—if we open ourselves to it—will lead us to love this world in the living of our lives.

I cannot give you your faith. Only you can find your own faith, your way of faith, your form of faith, the faith you stake your life upon. This is our choice: to live in faith, and so in hope, and with that faith and hope to act in love for this world, for those who are here and for those who are yet to be. Or, we can choose to live without faith, or to live with a faith that is not of this world, and so to feed the forces of hopelessness and apathy, death and destruction.

Our religious quest, our ultimate quest, is not to find a belief, but to find a way to experience the wholeness of our lives and the wholeness of the universe in which we are a minute speck. The heart of religion is personal experience. God, or the oneness or harmony of all that is, is not a matter of belief, but of experience. Emerson said that the question of whether one "believes in God" is an incomprehensible question: God is not something we "believe in" or not; God is an experience or presence accessible to us directly.

My alternative to traditional belief is faith. My faith is in the reality and the worth of this present moment and of each present moment. My religious call is to live in this present moment and in every moment of tomorrow as fully, morally, justly, enjoyably, and lovingly as I can. My accomplishments are modest indeed, and I have made many errors and wasted many hours, but the religious call is not to look back in remorse, but to move on to the next moment which calls.

This means that the great question for each of us is, what shall we do this moment with this great and incomprehensible gift of life which we have received?

a lifetime
in every
moment:
loving
the real

Look to this day!
For it is life, the very life of life.
In its brief course lie all the verities and realities
of your existence:
The bliss of growth,
The glory of action,
The splendor of beauty;
For yesterday is but a dream,
And tomorrow is only a vision;
But today, well lived, makes every yesterday a dream of happiness
And every tomorrow a vision of hope.
Look well, therefore, to this day.

-Kalidasa, 3rd c. Hindu poet, (often quoted by Senghas)

We live now, not in yesterday's hope for this day nor tomorrow's memory of this day. This day is sufficient for itself, and it waits for us to know it for itself, in its wonder, its depth, its eternity.

～

We must abandon the vanity of remorse and guilt for what we have failed in our past to achieve and abandon the distracting fantasies of what we may do tomorrow. Instead, let us turn to the only arena of life which exists for us: the moment now and here. With whatever our gifts and situations permit, let us live and act in this moment.

～

To live with passion does not mean to live irrationally. Passion and reason can be companions within the same person, just as passion can be compatible with responsibility and caring. To live passionately does not mean to live impulsively or irresponsibly, nor does it mean that we are to be frenzied or driven. Those who act compulsively are not able to enjoy the present moment, because they are driven by ghosts of the past or fears of the future.

To live with passion means to focus ourselves upon this present moment and each present moment. It is to live religiously, as Kierkegaard said, by bundling up all our uncertainties and fears and taking the leap of faith and trust in life, in the moment that is now. That call to a passionate commitment to life—which is at the heart of all religion—is one that has been made for thousands of years by poets as well as religious leaders.

To be able to live fully in the present moment is the most fundamental of all religious themes, because in order to do so we must be able to have faith in life, to trust life. Implicit in the call to live in this moment fully is the understanding that the heart of life is in the ordinary moments of life. Most of life is spent in very ordinary activities, and if we are to live with intensity we must live with intensity in those *ordinary* moments.

Indecisiveness and fear of failure or rejection are for many of us major barriers to living in the moment fully; another great barrier is our reluctance to acknowledge and to confront directly the pain in our lives. If we are to live fully in the world of this moment, we must be willing to open ourselves to the world as it is, the world as we experience it.

I have never known anyone (including myself) who has succeeded in getting over pain by trying to run away from it: it will run faster than we do and wait to surprise us at the next corner. I am not saying that pain is good, or that it should be cultivated, or that the experience of pain brings a necessary reward, as a kind of penitential suffering. Pain can be destructive indeed. I am saying that where there is pain in us, that pain will be our master until we are able to acknowledge its presence and its power. I have never found that I could appreciate the glory and beauty without from time to time also going through the discipline of facing the ugliness and pain.

William Wordsworth spoke of how he had learned to hear "the still, sad music of humanity" and to feel "a presence that disturbs with the joy" of something higher and deeper *[Lines Composed a Few Miles Above Tintern Abbey]*. That "still, sad music of humanity" plays for us too, and that joy waits for us too—if we have the spiritual discipline to prepare ourselves for it. An intense and passionate life waits for us, but it waits for us to unlock its glories with our own intensity and passion.

Let us exercise the courage to look at life as it truly is. May we see that our own lives are an inextricable mixture of good and bad, virtue and vice, success and failure, mortality and eternity. So may our vision be unclouded by ambition or self-deception of what we might wish to be or to appear to be, or the vain hope that the world is better than it is. Understanding our possibilities and our limitations, we must step forth each morning to a world that waits to hear our *yes,* a world that awaits our acts of loving participation.

~

The serenity of old age (a serenity that many old people never attain) is the ability to live in each moment as its comes and to relish it. The serenity of old age may look back and recall earlier times of happiness with those now dead, but it enjoys those memories as they are relived; it does not suffer pain in the nostalgia of their loss. Those who attain that serenity are free to live in the moment.

~

With the passage of each day of the limited number of days which is our lot, I am more and more aware of the preciousness of each passing moment, and that all that is required of us is to be fully alive in that moment, in moment after moment. If we are fully alive, we shall see what is there to be seen, we shall do what needs to be done, and we shall savor the gift of life.

Our salvation lies in this and in every moment, in our actions, in our contemplation of beauty, in our drinking a glass of water. As Thoreau said, "Do not stop to be scared yet; there are more terrible things to come, and ever to come." We are capable of living beyond a false confidence which tries to hide its eyes from reality and cowers in fear for the unknown future. We are capable of living in the confidence that says that I *can* be and I *will* be faithful to this moment, and to the moment after that, and to the moment after that, as long as there are moments. Millions before us have lived full lives in the face of evils and terrors beyond what we have known, and we are fully as capable as they were.

~

May we realize the preciousness of each moment, and not squander the gift of life in narrow pursuit of self-serving. Let us each find a way which will open our eyes, ears, minds, and hearts to the great reality that lies before us each moment, and so come to realize its greatness manifest in its beauty and its ugliness, its glory and its meanness. May we learn to say yes.

~

There are two fundamental attitudes toward the world which are possible for us. On the one hand, we can embrace life and existence; we can be open to the world as it is, fully recognizing its virtues and its many defects and depravities. On the other hand, we can choose to seek a permanent refuge from a troublesome world, to restrict our emotional openness and our caring to a few or to no one else; we can be a besieged defender of what we claim is ours alone. We can be, in other words, lovers of the world, or we can be lovers of only ourselves.

The great religions of the world have said that only those who are willing to care for the world as it is can be whole. If then we would be whole as persons, we must be lovers of the whole world and all its people We must live and work with the hope and the dream for a whole world that is itself a paradise of peace and justice for every man, and every woman, and every child.

~

Bob Fulghum, in *All I Need to Know In Life I Learned in Kindergarten,* said that "the biggest word of all" is *look*. Look *is* one of the big religious words: look and see with the eyes of a child. But looking is only one half of the religious way of life. We must look at the world and at ourselves, but seeing by itself is not enough. There is another word which must come after the looking, a religious word that demands from each of us all that we possess. That word is *yes*.

We must say *yes* to the world, after we have seen it and ourselves, as we really are. To say and to act with a *yes* is the ultimate religious call which the reality of our existence makes upon each of us. It is far easier to do that when five years old than when we have grown up to know the pain, injustices, and failures of the real world and of our own lives.

In addition, we must continue to make our *yes* in order for us to continue to *look*. If we cannot bear to affirm a world and a self that are a maze of virtue and vice, joy and pain, then we will not be able to bear to look with clear eyes at this playground our lives share. We must *look* and say *yes,* and *look* and say *yes,* again and again.

~

When we look with open eyes at what is before us we can make a full response. We can celebrate what we have, and we can work to make life better for ourselves and for others. If we are willing to look with open eyes, willing to look long enough and hard enough, we will know how to respond. We will see the evasions of our own minds and the bland bankrupt assurances of some of our political leaders. We will see past the old formulas and the old, tired ways of trying to deal with what we do not like, the foolish consistencies that fail to solve today's needs with yesterday's remedies. We will find new remedies beyond the old dogmas and patterns, new ways in which we can celebrate life and work for a healed world with a unified heart and mind.

～

When we accept the truth about this life and this world, we are free to live here and now. There is much that demands our life and our work:

- there are human beings to love, to cherish, and to mourn;
- there is pain and suffering to be eased;
- there are social problems to be faced;
- there are celebrations to be made of this life, and thanksgivings to be offered;
- there are children to be conceived and born and dedicated, to grow and take their place with us.

This is a real world, and we have the power to live real lives now and here. We who live in this time and place have been asked a question, and it is each of us who has the power to say *yes!*

～

The great mystics of history tell us that the experience of the religious is available to us in the daily, the mundane, the commonplace. That may indeed be true, but in order for us to realize its truth we must learn how to be aware it is there; the religious speaks to us in a language that we must learn. Just as we have to know how to listen to counterpoint in music so that Bach's music does not sound like disorderly noise but is revealed in all its greatness of part and whole, so we must learn to see what is already before us. There is a revelation before us, but we must be the revealers to ourselves.

Our busy daily lives and our mundane habits continue to tempt us to ignore what is real and to pursue distractions. I along with many others have idled away years in many ways, but today that does not matter. It does not matter what we did or did not do yesterday or last year. To absorb ourselves in a guilt for what we failed to realize or to do is to live still in the past, not the present; it is only another distraction from what we can realize today.

The infinite, the whole, the unity of the universe: none of those terms have any meaning if they have no meaning for each of us in this present moment. Even if we had not idled away many moments of the past, even if we had the realization of a Meister Eckhart, St. Teresa, St. John of the Cross, William Blake, or George Fox all rolled into one, that would not do anything for each of us today. As the third-century Hindu poet Kalidasa said, "Yesterday is but a dream, and tomorrow is only a vision. Look to this day! For it is life, the very life of life."

In other words, get out and enjoy the season! Go out and look for what it has to tell you about yourself! It will only have something to tell you if you go looking for it. To be worthy of the season and of ourselves we need to look at a tree or a leaf or the water of the lake and see it as though for the first time. If we are basking in the sun on a Sunday afternoon, we should make ourselves completely there on that Sunday afternoon, joined to that sunshine, not distracted by the thought that we will have to be back at work the next morning. When we do that, we are already back at work and not in touch with our present moment of immortality.

The only immortality we are able to enjoy is the immortality of the present moment in which we find ourselves. It was Emerson who noted that as soon as we become concerned with continuing our existence, we lose our immortality. As soon as we consciously try to hang on to something in the present moment, we are no longer in the present moment. We have lost at that moment our awareness that we are not separated from what is around us. If you want to save your life, lose it! Lose it in realizing what you already are! What you are right now is what you are made to be. Tomorrow you will be somebody else; let tomorrow's person realize what tomorrow will mean.

For everything there is a season, and the season of summer reminds us (if we are open to being reminded) that summer is to be enjoyed in summer and that life is to be enjoyed in life. Whatever life may mean, whatever joy it can give, whatever we have to experience, must be realized, understood, and felt in some present moment. We cannot enjoy a June day in December; not even our memory can give the awareness of what it means for us to be alive this very day. Whatever we realize today can only be realized today, and tomorrow will bring its own message when it becomes a today.

Seek, then, moments of solitude. Open yourself as you have never been open before to the harmony of which you are already a part. Do not just listen to the music—become the music. Become nature, the sky, the water, the mountains, the dawn, the sunset. Forget who you are. Forget that you are, and realize the great home of the universe in which you live. Have your immortality now. This time is made for you and you are made for it.

～

We review the past and remind ourselves of what might have been and is not, or of what was and is no longer. We look with anxiety to the future and fear that we shall not attain what we wish and will lose what we now have. So we miss the moment now and here. May we learn to live and to open our minds and senses to the wonder in this moment and this place.

～

I have come to agree with the apostle Paul's understanding of love as a state of being, not an action or feeling toward an object. This means if we love the real world as it is—love not only a few things or persons in the world but everything in the world (good and bad, caring and indifferent, friend and enemy, creation and destruction), love all that is, even though we become angry when innocent people suffer or when it does not seem just or fair—if we can still be in love with life, we can bear and endure whatever may happen to us and prevail.

I have known many who lived lives of faith, hope, and love despite deep misfortunes of loss, failure, betrayal, and illness. Those witnesses of faith, hope, and love do not tell us with their words; they show us with their lives. There is reason for the New Testament order of the words faith, hope, and love. Faith means trust, trust in the wholeness and health within us, and an affirmation of the world as it is, despite its shortcomings. That affirmation of wholeness and health is an act of faith that is necessary for us to make if we are to be whole.

With trust we can move to hope: hope to endure whatever life brings us, and beyond that, hope to live a life worth living. When we have trust and hope, then we are open to the ultimate affirmation of life—living in the love of life—which is its own reward and fulfillment. Loving the real world means loving all of the real world, loving it in its concrete goodness and evil. It is also what is called loving God. It is the only way to a full reconciliation with life and whatever life may bring.

～

I believe that our religious quest is to love and to know the world and those who are with us this very moment, not to question how or where we will be tomorrow. I believe that the concern for personal immortality or for the progress or immortality of our human race is a fruitless exercise in vanity.

Each of our lives is a personal pilgrimage. Our concern can be not the moral progress of the human race, but our own moral progress. Our concern can be not whether tomorrow or one hundred years from now an observer can note progress in history, but whether in our own lives we are acting to increase love and to ease and reduce suffering and injustice. To be distracted with anxiety over what happens after the death of our bodies or the death of our race is to be distracted from the glory of the world which has been given to us, and to which we have been given.

Every moment is sacred and calls for us to give it our trust. We do not need any guarantees of destiny nor of meaning. Destiny and meaning are in this very moment, and tomorrow's moment when tomorrow comes. My faith is in this moment, my hope is in this moment, my love is in this moment, God is in this moment. What more do we need?

~

If there is a Heaven, it is right here with us. If there is a Hell, it is here. The mystery of the everyday is in us and we are in it; it is directly ours beyond any abstraction.

~

winter of the spirit: times of darkness

The deepest meaning of Good Friday must be in the belief that all is lost. Without the depth of Good Friday the meaning of Easter is slight.

"Thy kingdom come, thy will be done." Those words are speaking to the experience of every person who sits in the ruin of his or her hopes and dreams, who faces failure or suffering or death, and who is then faced with the decision of whether to give up or to go on, to do what has to be done to the end. And the words "thy will be done" are the words of acceptance of that condition and the affirmation that we will go on to bear what has to be borne and to do what has to be done.

Every real prayer in the Christian tradition is essentially a prayer for strength to bear whatever may come, whether that prayer contains the theism of *not as I will, but as you will,* or whether it is a simple heartfelt *yes*. The Christian tradition understands that when we participate vicariously in the drama of Holy Week, we prepare ourselves for our own midnight vigils.

When T.S. Eliot writes of Good Friday, he does not hasten to reassure us with the promise of Easter. Darkness is darkness, and light is light. I have learned from Eliot that I do not have to be a Christian to know the drama of Holy Week, and I have come to believe that the real meaning of Holy Week is that there may not be an Easter. It is only in the absence of any assurance that the drama of Holy Week will conclude in a glorious Easter that that drama has its deepest meaning in the drama of our own lives. It is only in the absence of that assurance that we will be able to use that drama when we too sit one day in failure and hopelessness. That is when we too will be able to say, let what will be, be. That is when all we shall ask is for the strength and the understanding to go on to the end. That is the path to glory, as it leads in this world.

⤙

In a season of celebration we are struck with the poignant realization of how many lives around us are far from being able to celebrate. Many of us are in difficult and trying times, times of darkness, while around us everyone seems to be well off and happy.

May we find some consolation in remembering that the night of the soul is part of the human condition, and those who have known and will know the greatest light also know the greatest darkness; those with the greatest compassion will suffer the most and will do the most for others; those who have loved and who can love are the most bereaved. In the midst of our darkness may we remember and be sustained by our memories of the times of light in our past and by our hopes for our future engagement in life.

⤙

The religious question, said Harry E. Fosdick, is how do we find "the spiritual capacity to keep zest in living"? How are we able to believe in life? Learning itself does not confer zest in living or faith in life; there are multitudes of learned lost souls. Even health by itself does not confer zest in living: the presence of both physical and mental health by itself does not fill us with enthusiasm for life. So we come back to the question again: how are we able to believe in life?

One profound belief of Christianity is concerned not only with the power of death, but also with the power of death over us *in this life,* not in some life to come. That is, it is concerned with our being able to live the life we now have, without having life be under the shadow of death so that we are anxious and only half alive. The problem of being able to believe in life has always been the problem of not letting death have power over us, and as we get older this problem can become more acute, if we have not found some way to deal with it.

Our task is to live in this death-oriented world without letting death pollute us or have power over us. We are called to live a life of confidence and of inner freedom in the midst of this world without making changes in the external structure of the world the condition for our happiness.

To be a stoic is to decide to live within the shadow of death, to bear what has to be borne, and to do what has to be done, but without a fundamental zest or faith in life. It is to live without hope, unless it is merely the hope that the shadow will delay its further descent. Stoicism is one of our options.

The Christian answer is that it is possible to live outside the shadow of death in this life, but it requires a leap of faith. The Greek word for faith in the New Testament is also the word for trust; Christianity is saying that we must make a personal leap of trust into life. Whether it is through Christianity or some other route, there is no way except by a leap of trust, and we learn that from other human beings. Trust in life is passed from one human being to another: I cannot show you my faith by my words, but by my life. The founders of the great religions were those who somehow found faith in the life around them (when others did not see it) and transmitted that faith.

This is a season to be reminded of faith and trust, born and renewed. The flowers do not ask for faith to bloom; they simply bloom. We too—we who are aware of the power of death in life—have our time to bloom, but unlike the flowers, we must come to bloom through faith and trust in this life, to bloom in September as in May, to bloom here, now.

❦

We are surprised and shocked by the dark visions and impulses which sometimes arise within us. We are threatened by what we feel as forces of evil and disharmony around us. It is not easy to be reconciled to the dark side of ourselves.

May we understand that our feelings of fear, anger, temptation, and disharmony are part of our lives, and that our task is not to try to deny those feelings, but to resolve to deal with them. Our task is to bring forth the light of understanding, reason, and resolve, so that we can see what threatens us and follow the path to wholeness. May we know that within each of us is a source of strength and light which can restore us, if we open ourselves to it.

❦

We are conscious of the transiency of life as we perceive the transiency of nature. The summer is a particularly poignant time, because even as we glory in its lush greenness and warmth and beauty, we still feel in our bones the memory of the chill of winter, the wet cold of mud season, and the certainty of the seasons to come.

This is a season in which we may become most aware of the futility of any attempt to stop time, to prevent the ebb in the fullness of the flow. Winters lie before and behind us, whether we will them to or not. Let us hear and see and learn, and take the lessons of summer with us into the other seasons which await us.

In *Four Quartets* T. S. Eliot is telling us that in order for us to pass through our darkness, we must go by a way that is not ecstatic. We must go by a way which does not expect the ecstasy promised by the popular purveyors of a new birth. We must move through a valley in which we acknowledge that we have lost our way and are ignorant. Eliot says:

> We shall not cease from exploration,
> And the end of all our exploring
> Will be to arrive where we started
> And know the place for the first time.

"We shall not cease from exploration", we shall pursue our religious quest, "and the end of all our exploring"—the end of that quest—"will be to arrive where we started." The end of our search will be where we ourselves began (our birth, our openness to the world), and when we reach that place of a new beginning and new birth, then we shall "know the place for the first time." Then we shall understand our world and know it for the first time because we shall be able to comprehend it in all its good and evil, its beauty and ugliness, its health and its disease, its life and its death.

> Quick now, here, now, always—
> A condition of complete simplicity
> (Costing not less than everything)

"Quick now, here, now, always"—the chance to be reborn is always with us, always present. "A condition of complete simplicity," the simplicity that allows us to make a complete and open affirmation of life and the world—that kind of open affirmation is going to cost us "not less than everything." When we make that kind of affirmation, we lose the innocence of our spiritual childhood. We recognize and accept the fact that each of us will know suffering and darkness as well as joy and comfort; we accept that our friends and our flesh and blood will know that suffering and darkness too, as well as happiness. We will not exclude the tragedies from our consciousness, nor treat them as simple minuses in some addition process in which the pluses necessarily overbalance the minuses. If we are willing to pass through our own dark Advent, we shall be able to arrive at our destination.

⌣

Each of us now or later is troubled by anxiety, fear, and doubt. We are tempted by those religions and teachings which promise us tranquillity, the stilling of our fears, and certainty beyond doubt. But let us look not for someone or some faith that will save us from ourselves. Instead may we find the stilling of our troubled hearts in the knowledge and the trust that we are each part of one vast whole from which we came, in which we now live and move and have our being, and into which we shall merge when we die. No longer blinded by our fears and petty defenses, let us see the real as it is, in all its joys and sorrows, its glory and its depravity, and move in ways which help and heal ourselves and others.

⌣

Death is as natural as life; life and death are part of the same process. There is no death without life, the life that dies, and there is no life without death. If we place a taboo in our own minds to thinking about death, then we are denying as much a part of our nature as if we were to refuse to acknowledge our sexuality. It is time that we acknowledge our mortality as well as our sexuality. Since both life and death are part of reality, and the religious quest must include the search for truth, for what is real, then our religious quest must include a look at death as well as life.

I often say that at a wedding "everybody gets married": those who are married think about their own marriage; those who are yet to be married ponder their future; those who are divorced and widowed think about their past marriage and their future. Likewise, at memorial services and funerals, everybody experiences death: we think about what might be—the death of someone close to us and our own death. It is our very presence at those services which allows us not only to celebrate the life of the one who has died and to mark the event of that death, but also to celebrate the worth of our own lives, seen in the frame that nature has given us between the boundaries of birth and death. Every funeral, every memorial service, every committal service, is in part for another and in part for ourselves, a celebration of another and a celebration of ourselves.

~

Our aspirations are often beyond our grasp, and we know the taste of failure and remorse. May we accept the sense of failure as an inescapable part of the moral part of our character, knowing that the courage to try must include within it the courage to fail, and knowing that our pilgrimage through life must be made by taking two steps forward and one backward.

~

There are regular conditions of human experience we have to struggle with which tell us that things are hopeless, and a voice inside us says time and again, "What's the use?" What each of us must have, in order to sustain ourselves against a world which urges us to hopelessness, is faith. We must have a faith of some form. That faith may be different for each of us, and it may not be faith in any traditional religious form. It may be Christian or non-Christian, theist or non-theist, but whatever form that faith takes, it must be an affirmation against the darkness and experiences of defeat, an affirmation that somehow our life has meaning when we act morally.

We must have faith that acts of caring and compassion are worth doing, despite the fact that they will not bring an end (by themselves) to human suffering, faith that the creation of beauty is a gift we can make to life without having to expect a clear reward, faith that we each have the power to heal wounds of others, although we cannot conquer all hurt.

We seek a faith that will inspire us and lead us to move closer to a better world by what we do or leave undone. Unless we have some kind of faith, we will not be able to have a life which can sustain adversity and face our daily world. Men and women have been able to continue as functioning and caring human beings as long as they had some kind of faith in something larger than their own lives. This has been true even when that faith may have violated reason. It is possible to live by an irrational faith, but it is not possible to live without hope, and hope requires faith.

Our faith is built in some way upon a confidence that reality is larger than any one of us, larger than we can ever know personally. This does not mean that faith is irrational, but that our reason and experience are not sufficient to provide that faith. "Therefore," as it says in Hebrews, "lift your drooping hands and strengthen your weak knees," for each of us, every day, has the choice: we can sink in the conviction of futility, or we can swim by our faith.

In its beauty and its harshness, in its warmth and chill, its splendor and its squalor, the world we live in answers with silence our yearnings for justice and goodness. We face the certainty of our death without knowledge or assurance to sustain us. We try to create gods who will give us sustenance in our dark hours, but the gods that we create become only idols in our own images.

Yet the world about us gives us clues, if we will understand them. Let us approach our dark hours with a trust that will open our eyes to read the handwriting of Creation that is there for all to see, written by a power that is directed by no mere human need or yearning, but which sustains and unfolds the vast cosmos in which we play our little parts.

⤛

We cannot expect to eliminate fear or anxiety, but we can remove the power of that fear to destroy our lives. It is, for example, an essential part of the human condition that we are anxious about death, and if we insist on trying to avoid that anxiety, we shall become captive of it. It is only when we acknowledge that, yes, we are afraid of dying, that we are able to live fully. The "peace which passes understanding" of the Christian tradition does not refer to the peace of death, but to the peace which can come to us in life when we accept the anxieties of living.

⤛

We are in the darkest time of the year, as we approach the winter solstice, and a sense of gathering darkness grows in us, as it does each year. We are in the time of deepest darkness and despair, the time when the *need* for a Messiah is most deeply felt, the dark part of the cycle.

These cycles of despair and rebirth occur throughout the year in us; it is only that they are dramatized at this time of year, and in their dramatization we perceive what they are telling us about our experience at many other times. We have come to acknowledge the dark side of the human soul and the dark side of the world in which we live, a darkness which is not simply the absence of light, but a dark presence within ourselves which shows itself from time to time.

Ours must be not only a religion of light, but a religion for our times of darkness. The way of religion is not a way around the darkness; the way of religion is the way through the darkness. There is no way around. In T.S. Eliot's words (in *Four Quartets*), "I said to my soul, be still, and let the dark come upon you which shall be the darkness of God." That does not mean that we throw ourselves into a pit of depression and despair and give up. It means that when we know that darkness, we carry on and we wait.

> I said to my soul, be still, and wait without hope
> For hope would be hope for the wrong thing; wait without love
> For love would be love of the wrong thing; there is yet faith
> But the faith and the love and the hope are all in the waiting.

We cannot see into the darkness of our own souls, but we wait. Something is happening. As Eliot says, it is like the time in the theater, when the house lights and the stage lights are completely extinguished, and we encounter complete blackness. We wait, and we hear the faint movement of the scenery as it is being changed, and we know that when the lights do at last come on again, we shall be in a new place. We do not know what that new place will be until the lights come on again, and so we must wait and wait while we sense something invisible happening to us.

The times of Advent in our lives are those times when we wait in the darkness, when we are void of feeling and void of understanding. There are times when there is only the waiting.

> You say I am repeating
> Something I have said before. I shall say it again.
> Shall I say it again? In order to arrive there,
> To arrive where you are, to get from where you are not,
> You must go by a way wherein there is no ecstasy.
> In order to arrive at what you do not know
> You must go by a way which is the way of ignorance.

In order to possess what you do not possess
You must go by the way of dispossession.
In order to arrive at what you are not
You must go through the way in which you are not.
And what you do not know is the only thing you know
And what you own is what you do not own
And where you are is where you are not.

What is it for which we are waiting? We are waiting for a birth
in us of something new. So it is not a coincidence that Advent is
represented by the time of Mary carrying the child who is growing
in the darkness toward the time of birth. We are each of us part of
the darkness. We are each of us Mary with our unseen life within us.

This is the time when we must wait, when we must be ready,
the time when the changes are taking place in the darkness. There
will be light to come, and there will be a birth for you, a birth
from you, and a birth within you.

꒰ꜜ

When we are tired or broken in spirit, there is a power
accessible to us which can renew and restore us to wholeness.
That power does not come to us from some alien god lowered
onto our human stage by wires; that power comes through us
and is exercised by our own will. We may have differing
understandings as to the nature and source of that power, but
we each have access to it. We are the instruments of that
power, if we will use it. What is at stake then is whether you
and I will use the opportunity that exists before us.

꒰ꜜ

There is newness within each of us that is waiting to be born, new revelations within ourselves, waiting to be revealed. The way through the darkness is by dispossessing ourselves of our attachments to ideas, possessions, experiences, memories. We are to become again as little children. We must live without regret or nostalgia for our past, for the past cannot be recreated, not even in our memories in ways that will bring life to us again. We must live without regret that there are many loved ones who were once with us in our childhood and in our maturity who are no longer with us. We feel their absence, but our regret does not bring them back to us nor bring light back into our lives.

There are many among us who have passed through darkness and emptiness and found a rebirth of life and hope and love, who have known a Christmas morning in their adult lives. Christmas waits for us, but only if we wait for it, only if we become as children again, empty and open to receive the gift of life. "Truly, I say to you, unless you turn and become like children, you will never enter the kingdom of heaven." (Matthew 18:3) Christmas waits for us, but only if we wait for it.

⌒

As we enter the season which celebrates the rebirth in us of life and light, we are reminded of our need for a rekindling of faith and hope and love. At this time we become especially aware of the darkness in our own lives and in the lives of those around us.

As the night is succeeded by dawn, as the time of shorter days and longer nights is to change and our days will begin again to lengthen, so in our own lives we will pass through the dark hours, if we persist in our faith and hope in the waiting. Within each of us is the spirit of rebirth and dawn and springtime, if we wait for it and are ready for it.

May we remember that dawn will not come to us if we stay with eyes closed: only those who wait and look at the dark will see the dawn.

—

Each of us must have developed for ourselves some sense of the continuity of our life in something larger than ourselves that lasts beyond our death, in order for us to remain mentally healthy, to be open to the religious dimension in life, and to come to terms with our own mortality. Or, to put it in a negative way, unless we each see our life as part of something which goes on after we die, we risk our mental health, we impoverish our religious life, and we become enslaved to the fear of death, particularly as we get older. Without some such sense of continuity we are going to be slaves to our own death.

I am sustained by two ways of understanding: that I am part of a vast universe that rolls on through eternity, whose parts take ever changing forms, including my own brief visit to life; that my contemplation of that universe and that eternity gives me all the mundane ecstasy I need, in silence, in the forms of beauty, and in my making music before it.

—

Each of us has known pain and suffering and loss, and when we have hurt, we have not expected our friends to stop the pain, but to be with us in the compassion of their presence. When we become angry with what has happened to us, though we may curse our misfortune, let us not expect the intervention of some outside force to heal us magically. Instead, let us look to the power that lies accessible within each of us, the power to greet and celebrate our good fortune when it is good, and to face and endure our bad fortune. We seek not a fantasized cure, but the strength to endure, and with that endurance, to prevail.

—

Our basic principle as wintry spirits, as opposed to those who are summer spirits, is that when we face the uncertainties of life, when we know doubt, pain, loneliness, and the presence of death, we do not turn away. The summer spirit turns away from uncertainty and doubt to affirm his or her certainties of faith, but we turn toward those uncertainties. We have come to know that if we are not willing to live through that winter of the spirit, there will be no spring for us. We do not romanticize emotional pain, nor are we masochistic. It is simply that we have found that when we try to avoid confronting a painful situation head on and try to suppress it, that pain never goes away. It stays there at the edge of our consciousness, casting a cloud over our lives and tainting every one of our affirmations. We have found that the only way to emerge into the light is not to try to escape the darkness, but to go through the darkness.

I call this process of turning toward our pain *letting go.* We let go of the vain hope that we can escape the pain. We let go of the image we have tried to have of ourselves as someone who is faultless or invulnerable, who cannot be hurt, who is always adequate. We let go of the myths about ourselves that we have cherished and the dreams and hopes that have been shattered. It is only after we have let go of those images, dreams, and fantasies that we are able to see ourselves as we really are; it is only then that we begin to be able to reaffirm our life in the real world.

Those shattered myths, fantasies, and hopes will be ghosts which haunt us until we bury them, and the way we bury them is to face the truth that they are indeed dead myths, fantasies, and hopes. Letting go does not make us less than we were; it does not diminish us. We have already lost what is to be lost; letting go means abandoning our illusion that we are not diminished. We have lost something we had when we fail in our work, or when a friendship is broken, or when we realize that we have personal defects or inadequacies which disturb us. But letting go will restore us to our selves, to our real and diminished selves, and unless we are restored to our real selves, we cannot be restored to the real world.

When I have failed to be what I want to be or to do what I had hoped to do, when I have lost what I wished to keep, then I am indeed less than I was: I am diminished. I have only one arm, where before I had two arms. But I will let go of that image of myself as a person with two arms. I will be a whole person with one arm. Only when I know myself as someone with one arm can I truly know myself, and only then can I be whole and at home with myself in the real world.

We can be freed of the power of death over us only if we let go of our need to believe we are immortal, if we let go of our picture of ourselves as always alive. If we are to escape the dread of death, we must die to our own selves. Only then can we live out from under that shadow. If we try to hang on to our life—to *save* it — we shall lose our life in this and each present moment we have left to live, and if we let go or *lose* our life, we are freed to be here in each moment we have.

This process of dying to one's self, in order to live in the fullness of the present moment, is the final part of our letting go of the bonds which can bind us. It is the final farewell to those false or dead dreams, hopes, and fantasies that we have created, in whose bondage we remain until we let them go.

Finally, to be freed of the prison we make for ourselves by our false or dead hopes and dreams means that we can live with the treasures of our own memories. We can look back without regret or remorse at the succession of men and women we have loved, and at the succession of persons we ourselves have been. We can let go of any fantasy to believe that they are alive with us, or that we need them now to be who we are now. We were diminished when we lost those we loved, but we are whole today, and we live not with them but with our loving memory of them.

It is easy to affirm life in the light and the warmth of day, in the beauty of the seasons, in the love of family and friends. It is much more difficult to affirm life when we are in the shadow of disappointment, suffering, and the absence of others who care, when the facts are unfriendly.

May we find within ourselves the spirit which is already within each of us, the spirit which gives us the courage to affirm life in all its goodness and its sadness. Let us proceed with courage, seeking not to pretend the world is as it is not, nor seeking magical relief from the burdens of life. Rather, let us seek the fortitude to sustain those burdens, and desire not to escape life but to exercise our will and our strength to live.

↫

We must burrow deeply for the quality of life which makes the rest of life worthwhile. We have buried our religious spirit deep within ourselves, and we are going to have to burrow down and bring it back out. Despite all we may have done to bury what is best within ourselves, that spirit is still there if we are willing to go after it amid the distractions of our busy world.

If the flame of life is low, and if the winds of the world threaten to extinguish it, let us cup our hands over that flame to protect it. Let us look to our inner life to feed the flame until it flares again, not some dim reflection of the life of our youth but a living, renewing, and present flame. When that flame returns to fullness, let us be ready to take it to bring light to those around us and to a dark world.

To the life that is in us, to the future that is in us, to the spirit of renewal that waits for us, though we walk through the valley of the shadow of death, we shall trust in your presence within us, and we shall know you again. We are open to your power.

↫

We pass through a time of doubt and trial. Let us reject the false prophets who would give us a heart easy in wrath and an arm cruel in retribution. May we be more concerned with understanding the anger of others than in punishing that anger. Let us have the strength to be gentle, the courage to be un-angry, and the inner security to hear the truth, so that we each may be bearers of the spirit of life and truth and love.

Both Buddhism and Christianity contain elements in their traditions which recognize that if we are to be able to continue to live fully in the presence of the realities of our own mortality and suffering and the mortality and suffering of others, we must go through some kind of experience in which we die to our old selves. We must give up trying to hang on to the fiction that we can avoid the reality of physical death and suffering by ourselves and every other human being. If we do not confront that reality directly, we live a lie.

This does not mean that we should spend most of our lives consciously contemplating the truth of death and suffering, but it means that if we do not confront that truth, then whatever we do is done with a shadow over it. We can try to run from that reality, but it will pursue us wherever we go and come to cast a larger and larger shadow over our lives, until and unless we turn and confront it directly. It is not morbid for us to confront death and suffering as real death and real suffering; what is morbid is for us to pretend that they do not exist. When we make that avoidance because of our fear, our fear becomes our master. We can be freed to enjoy the real world, as it is, only when we are willing to open our eyes and ears and hearts to everything that is true about that real world.

Letting go does not mean that as we give up our old self with all its ego-needs, we shall cease being subject to the pains or the joys of life. On the contrary, the joys will be more joyful, because they will be unclouded by anxiety, and the pains will be more clearly recognized, because they will not be disguised by our fears and evasions.

Truth cuts through the masks of joy and of pain, and we can let truth liberate us from the illusion that there is any ultimate security, except the security that comes when we embrace the impermanence of all things. Jesus and the Buddha and Henry David Thoreau tell us that if we let go of all our false fantasies of security, and embrace this great, living, impermanent world as it is this very moment, then we shall be freed to enjoy and to rejoice in this wonderful, beautiful world. Then we shall also receive the gift of grace, which is the power to prevail over the suffering, evil, and death in this terrible, ugly world, until the time we have been granted here as visitors runs its course.

❧

We are liberated when we realize that we are not going to be able to avoid failure. We have had to choose at many forks in the road and to follow one path rather than another, which we now believe might have been better. Life has not been what we thought or dreamed it would be. But when we realize that to live is to fail in many ways, when we ourselves have tasted failure and disappointment, we are able to be more compassionate, rather than angry, in the face of the failure of others, and more accepting, rather than blaming. We are able to live more fully in the present rather than be tormented with the errors of the past or seduced by the fantasy of some perfect future.

❧

The glory of the earth and the bright sun are sometimes a reproach to our dull and listless spirits. In the times when we labor under doubt and dullness of spirit, may we live in trust that we shall pass through the shadows and know once again the inner fire and the light within. As our faith in life has sustained us and been fulfilled in us in the past, so that faith will carry us again from dark to light. Let us go forward with the courage and confidence of that faith.

BECOMING WHO WE ARE:

the mystery of our own being

Part of the gift of consciousness we have received is our awareness of our separation from the world and the source from which everything has come. Let us restore ourselves from our state of separation by facing directly the mystery of our own being.

～

In the midst of the everyday we are diverted and absorbed in the busyness of living. We take no time to look, to listen, and to wonder at the miracle that is about us and within us. When we are surfeited with the details of work and home and with our cares, too often we seek respite only through diversion and entertainment.

When we have had our fill of cares, and when we have found that our spirit finds no solace nor renewal in our pursuit of diversion, let us turn to the true solace, the source of renewal within each of us: the silence which speaks and the solitude which can be our true companion. So may we come to know who we are and to be truly at home in the world.

~

We were each born with the potential to realize certain powers of supreme importance, and our process of becoming who we are is a process of learning to nurture, develop, and utilize those skills and powers. We were born with the potential to be able to celebrate life, to act with caring for others, to have a passion for justice and truth, to affirm life despite our inevitable suffering and death—the potential not only to labor, but to live, enjoy, love, worship, to embrace existence itself and everything in it, including everything that was here before we were born and that will be here after we are gone.

~

Unlike all other life on earth, which is driven by necessity, we are the creatures who have learned how to choose what roles we shall play in the course of our existence. In the midst of the complicated dance we have learned to perform, may we turn within to listen to the voice of our deepest self, which has its own song to sing and its own dance to do. Let us be concerned with what is real within us, rather than with what others may perceive we are or want us to be. In a world which would make us in its image, may we be ourselves.

~

We are constantly being given clues when we are out of touch with our inner lives. It is in others' eyes that we see ourselves reflected, if we are willing to look even when we are not sure we shall like what we see. Clues are also received from within ourselves: we find ourselves responding with anger or impatience when there seems little to be angry or impatient about, or we become depressed, suspicious, or filled with stress, ready to defend ourselves against some unrecognized inner threat of exposure of our weaknesses or failings.

Once we become aware of our disharmony and have gotten in touch with our real feelings—whether we do that with the help of others or by ourselves—then we need to identify what it is within us that is causing that disharmony. If we accept the truth about ourselves, we are restored to ourselves and can move forward, but if we deny the truth about ourselves, we have entered a way of life that is built upon falseness. If we are false to ourselves, how can we be true to anyone else? We must accept ourselves as we are in order to live with ourselves in the real world.

～

We address our own innermost hearts, to search within to know how better to pursue the highest and the best within us. We would lay bare the patterns and pretense we make to others and to ourselves, the habit and conformity, the immaturities left from childhood and the weariness of an old age too early and too willingly accepted.

May we look with courage and hope at our own inner souls, and act in resolution to cure the evils of our world and of ourselves. Let us act neither in simple obedience nor defiance of any authority outside us, but with the strength and authority that is within our own hearts.

～

Ralph Waldo Emerson understood that many of those who attack social conformity become newly enslaved by a conformity to their own variety of *non*conformity. He understood that conformity comes not from outside ourselves, but from within ourselves: it comes from our attempt to make ourselves conform to an image of ourselves we willingly adopt as our own. The only real conformity is self-conformity, our constant glances in the mirror to see whether in fact we look the way we want to be seen.

～

Let us address the spirit within each of us which, if we will open to it, mirrors our shortcomings and calls us to a higher, more noble life. May we listen to the promptings of that spirit in the voice of our conscience. Let us be concerned, not with our faults, limitations, and shortcomings, but rather with how we may henceforth act toward others and ourselves so that neither we nor they become victims of what we do or say. Let us be less concerned with what in the past we have done or left undone and more concerned with what we may now do or avoid doing. In this way may we become free from the burden of self and become instruments of light, justice, and love.

～

Each of us is the incarnation of the spirit of life: if the Messiah is to live in us, it is each of us who must be the Messiah, it is each of us who is the Messiah. Within each of us is the Messiah waiting to be born, after the time of waiting in the darkness. There must be times of waiting in the darkness, but there is something alive in us, waiting to be born.

～

Avarice is most often thought of as the desire to hoard money, but it is much broader and more insidious than that. It is at heart an attachment to objects: the person infected by avarice identifies himself or herself with possessions. Those possessions may be money or its representation in bankbooks and stocks and bonds, or it may be in a house or land. Avarice may even be found in the attachment and identification a person has to a vista or view.

There is an insidious incentive in our society to avarice, to an acquisition of property to which we become unduly attached. The absence of a secure inherited social position in our country means that we are defined by most Americans by our property: "He's the fellow who owns the Mercedes," or "She's the person in the brick house on the hill." Even our ethnic identities give way to that democracy of the dollar. Money, income, and property in our country are an index both of our security against vicissitudes and of our status.

There are advantages and disadvantages in this situation. A democracy in which success is based upon property and level of income—if it is coupled with equal opportunity of access to that income—offers a healthier system than most other alternatives, such as an oligarchy of a few wealthy families, an aristocracy, or a caste system. Most of the criticism of our system is over the issue of equal opportunity of access, the denial of full access to property and income because of race or sex. Every system has it special sins as well as its special virtues, and one of our system's problems is that it encourages the development of avarice.

The amount of money or wealth we have is no reliable indication of how avaricious we may be. The issue is not the amount of our property, but our attitude toward it: do I own my property, or does it own me? Every one of us here is a rich person, and our attachment to our possessions is a trap.

One of the most insidious forms of avarice is our excessive attachment to habit—often a disguised form of attachment to our possessions—and habit tends to get worse as we get older. So, for an occasional intrusion upon our attachments to habits and possessions we should be thankful, for they are warnings to us against becoming enslaved to ourselves.

Avarice, or the clinging to habits and possessions, is not as dramatic as some of the other of the seven deadly sins, but it can be just as destructive, and it is insidious. So I ask you a question which only you can answer for yourself: what would be the hardest thing for you to let go—what possession, habit, idea, or power? The answer to that question will tell you what is your master.

~

We are pilgrims on the journey of life, and as we go along our pilgrimage we seek at each point to examine whether we are pursuing truth or only the name of truth, goodness or only the appearance of goodness, honesty with ourselves or merely a self-deception which wears the mantle of self-candor.

May we seek to be disturbed in our illusions and refusals to see and to be reminded of the real world of suffering which cries out for our help. Let us renew our commitment to make our lives not a retreat from disturbing truths, but part of a larger life.

~

If we want to know what kind of ego it is to which we are personally attached, we only need to ask ourselves what it is that makes us feel defensive. What comment cuts us to the quick? What criticism of us rouses our anger? Each of us has our own list, and that is the list of our ego attachments, the list of what we depend upon others to supply to us, in order for us to feel verified as a person.

The death of the self makes us as alive as it is possible to be as human beings. The great spiritual leaders of history show us what spiritual energy can be liberated when the self is liberated by the elimination of its need to be verified. With that personal liberation we become truly free to return to the world, to act and to do and to be, free of self-serving demands, free to be caring, free to enjoy what there is to enjoy. Pain will still be pain, but it will be physical or mental suffering or the pain of compassion, without the pain of a threatened or damaged ego.

~

We are but dimly conscious of the glory and the nobility that lie within each of us. We pretend we lack a higher nature and the power to elevate our lives. We submerge the best in us for the sake of the approval and the acceptance of others, and so reduce ourselves to a meaner life.

May we follow the good conscience which comes only from within us. Let us follow the inspiration of our own nature and be an encouragement to others to seek the highest and the best within themselves, though that may lead them from common ways.
So may we let shine the divine lamp that was lighted in each of us when we became part of the living world.

~

Whatever our faith or sense of harmony, we need to test ourselves by our works. If I am uncaring and do nothing for anything outside myself, then I am living by an immoral faith, no matter how blissful and happy that faith may make me feel.

The great likelihood for error is in our tendency toward moralism. We need to remind ourselves that even when we serve the noblest causes of peace and reconciliation—even when we attack the great evils of racism and hunger—we are susceptible to drying up as spiritual persons and becoming moralistic bigots. To prevent our moral actions from degenerating into a barren moralism we must feed our spiritual lives.

We must open ourselves to the awareness of a universe that is one unity, whole and good, of which we are part. That universe is benign, and it is also cruel and indifferent. It is beautiful and ugly, caring and uncaring. But with all its goodness and its evil—in its wholeness—it is good, and in it there is a harmony that takes us all in, all of us in our joy and pain, life and death. Our consciousness of that unity and that harmony is the food which feeds our faith and trust as we go on our way between birth and death.

～

We live in a familiar world of everyday, of warm and cold seasons, of friends and ceremonies of daily life. But we know that ours is a middle world: within us and around us is a world of energy and matter whose presence is felt but not seen, and beyond us and the stars is yet another vast world that dwarfs all human existence and knowledge.

May we come to feel part of those larger and smaller worlds, and know that they too are part of each of us. Then, being restored to our home in the universe, let us work to make our small place and our short life one of peace, love, and justice.

～

There can be immense personal satisfaction in fulfilling a role. The sense of worth and accomplishment can be substantial when we use our skills, work our trade or occupation, maintain a home, play our part. In addition to paying for our groceries and a roof over our heads, the fulfilling of our roles can be of great value to others. What that role will be for a particular person varies, for what some love to do, others abhor doing, but the critical decisions of our lives include our choice of roles.

To be simply players of roles in the theater of life, however, is not enough for us, for there is another side to life which we must not slight: the world of the self, the world in which we are present to ourselves and to a few others simply as a human being both greater and simpler than the collection of personas we have to wear. Most of us need the encouragement of a few people close to us to step out of our roles when we are with them and to be strengthened to be ourselves. In addition, we need to have a healthy sense of self in order to handle criticism from others about the way we are performing our roles.

We can live in this world, we can grow in our lives, we can pass through the valley of the shadow of death, if we know how to let go of the idol we have made of our own person. If we try to hang on to an image we would like to think we are, we are lost. If we try to believe we are simply the roles we play, we are hollow. There is flesh and blood beneath these suits and neckties and dresses! If we are willing to lose the image of ourselves which we have been perfecting, we can save the life within ourselves.

~

When we contemplate the vast array of stars, separated from us by distances and times beyond the understanding of our ordinary thought, we feel ourselves to be insignificant specks in an incomprehensible universe. As we learn more and more of the world within each cell of life, each molecule and atom, we are overwhelmed by the complexity and the structures beyond the range in which we live our daily lives.

In our awe for those evidences of worlds beyond our understanding, may we know that we are one with them. Though we are
flawed, our presence here on earth is as glorious a flowering as any
other part of Creation, and we have each received the precious and
unique gift of the consciousness of our own life. We know that
there was a time when we were not; we know that we are; and we
know that there will be a time when we shall not be. That
knowledge is a burden that we accept with solemn joy.

~

In times of solitude may we search within ourselves to come to
know our own impulses and feelings, to be intimate with what is
most intimate to us, our self. Let us come to understand that it is
not our feelings, thoughts, and impulses which determine what we
are and what we are to be, but what we decide to *do* with ourselves
and with others in the presence of those feelings, thoughts, and
impulses. Knowing ourselves, may we act on what we deem worthy and avoid what we consider unworthy, and so come to be for
others a resource in trouble and a companion in joy.

~

Despite our sincere aspirations to be good and to do good,
we are human, and we retain our human aggressions and emotions.
It is our very aspirations to goodness that seduce us into doing or
condoning evil under the name of goodness. We do not need to
fear evil as evil. We have always been ready to defend ourselves
against evil that appears under the name of evil. What we need to
fear in ourselves and in others is evil that appears in the name of
goodness.

There is no ideal or cause worthy of support which is not susceptible to abuse, corruption, or perversion—the more ideal, the
more susceptible to abuse. The greatest cruelties in history have
been committed in the name of religion, the greatest repressions in

the name of liberty, the greatest betrayals of country in the name of patriotism. We have committed our most selfish acts to those closest to us in the name of love.

Let us aim, as Thoreau said, above morality. We will not try simply to be good—that is the refuge of the cold moralist and the zealot. We shall "be good for something" and for somebody. All ideals finally "come between us and the light." Let us so act in harmony with the needs of our earth and its people that we are instruments of a force higher and deeper than any words or ideals. Despite our failures and our lapses we shall break the cycle of judgment: we shall learn to cease judging the judgers and hating the haters. Thus may we become true instruments of peace and love beyond the words of peace and love.

~

We are in danger of becoming pre-occupied with our illness or limitations and of becoming victims of the tyranny of our own preoccupation. That does not mean that we should deny any limitation, sorrow, or loss we have suffered. The path to health requires that we recognize what has been changed beyond repair and what is still within our power to change and to cure. What is required of us is that we have the wisdom to know our own power.

~

Most of us have times of spiritual health and times of spiritual sickness. A person who is spiritually healthy is someone who is living in harmony with the world and with oneself, while seeing the world and the self realistically. Being whole includes the ability to sense the value of one's own life and the value of the lives and things around us, and being healthy includes our participation in the world around us, our response as a harmonious part of that larger world.

~

In order for us to be healed, to live in the real world, to live with our real selves, we must confess to ourselves when we have made mistakes, and we must acknowledge to ourselves our strengths and weaknesses, our talents and imperfections. We cannot be at home in the world if we are not at home with ourselves. That is not to say that in retrospect we approve of everything we have done or left undone, but that we accept the truth, the reality of what we have done or left undone. We do not ignore who we are, or try to lie to ourselves by willing to deny who we are. Only through self-confession can we be free to be who we are.

What does it mean, *each of you is made in the image of God?* It does not mean that God is some being that exists somewhere in human form; it means that within your human form with all its faults, shortcomings, and mental and physical limitations, in your being, in your self, is wholeness. You are whole despite all infirmity or age. As Carl Jung said, God represents wholeness for us. To be made in the image of God is to receive the gift of wholeness from the moment we become a human being.

The act of faith which waits for each of us is our acceptance of the gift of our wholeness. We are already whole, but we must realize that wholeness. We must begin by confessing to ourselves exactly who we are. We must accept and forgive ourselves for not being perfect, and free ourselves from the bonds that have bound us since we were children. The people who placed the burden of our conviction that we are inadequate cannot remove that burden from us; only we can free ourselves.

Take those old tapes off that tell you are weak. Put them into cold storage, and put on the tape which reminds you that you have been made in a divine image. Cast off the yoke your father and mother put on your shoulders, whether they intended to burden you or not. Live in faith—faith in your wholeness, faith in yourself.

humbled
by reality

A person who is moral is not someone who is perfect.
Perfection has never existed in the flesh. Rather, a moral
person is one who is conscious of the possibility of doing
wrong, or of indifference and uncaring, and who is nevertheless
committed to being a caring, faithful, and good person.
A moral person is one who is sensitive to wrong in oneself,
and when one is wrong, to correct it and to abstain from
that wrong.

~

We are grateful for the gift of being able to see ourselves in the
light of the truth about ourselves, to see the reflections of our
imperfections, to be aware of the differences between the reality of
ourselves and the ideal portrait we would paint of ourselves. The
gift of seeing ourselves is an imperfect one, for our fears and shame
distort our mirror of reality; there are times when it is too painful
for us to look directly upon ourselves.

Yet, we are thankful for that gift of self-consciousness, for it is our way to a better life for ourselves and others. We seek not to torture ourselves with the painful knowledge of our shortcomings, but to use that self-knowledge as a means to be mended and restored to the way of truth and honesty. We are grateful then for the gift of the mirror of the soul.

Unless we are ready to acknowledge that there is much we do not know, we shall never learn more than we know now. May we remember that unless we are able to recognize our errors, we shall never be free to correct them. Unless we recognize that truth, conscience, and love are as accessible to our neighbor as they are to us, we shall never be able to do unto our neighbor as we would be done unto. So, in our ignorance we shall learn; from our error we shall be restored to truth and goodness; in our humility we shall be exalted.

The life of the spirit, wherever it has flourished, requires humility, and we have been humbled by reality. We have learned that there is no royal road—not even a liberal royal road—to being a whole person. We have learned that if we are to be whole persons, we do not become whole simply by taking courses in how to be a good friend or lover or parent, just as we do not become a musician simply by taking music lessons. All that study can help us only if we bring ourselves wholly and willingly to our encounter with life and see ourselves first in all our strengths and weaknesses, ready to learn, ready to be a pilgrim to wholeness.

It is not enough for us to be in touch with our feelings of anger and sexuality, of love and compassion: we must learn how to transform those feelings into acts of caring for others and for ourselves. As we are humbled by our awareness of our shortcomings and self-deceptions, and the cruelties of our nation and world, we create the means of our restoration to wholeness. We become inspired to be whole because we sense the gulf between our present state and a wholeness that lies beyond us. We have the power to become whole because we are inspired by the vision and the presence of wholeness.

Only those who know they are sick can be cured; only those who understand they are broken will be made whole. There is hope for us because we can be open to sense the power of wholeness and our need for it; there is hope for us because we know we are broken and wish to be whole. Blessed are the humble, for they shall inherit the earth.

⌣

Let us seek in our religious search not only a solace from the bruises of life, but a challenge to be better persons. Remember that the times when we are most wrong will be the times when we are sure we are most right. Let us be open to the source of new light, new understanding, and new forgiveness of our failures, so that we are concerned—not with what we may have done right or wrong, nor how good or bad we have been—but with how caring and how just we *shall be.* So may we inherit the future of the life left to us, and not become buried alive by our own past.

⌣

We must continue the process of self-confrontation. We no longer use the term "original sin," but we continue to keep the understanding of the human condition expressed in those words, the awareness that we have "the infinite human capacity for self-deception," as Reinhold Niebuhr said. Rather than "original sin" we have used the word "doubt." We believe that doubt is a necessary adjunct to faith, for it protects us from our own self-righteousness and moralism, protects us from a new dogmatism, and keeps our eyes and minds open.

Let us then be doubters and believers at the same time, struggling to live in love and to act in truth and justice, while we walk humbly in the presence of the spirit which speaks to us of absolute truth, selfless love, and merciful justice.

⤙

We have given and received acts of generosity and good will in our personal lives and in the life of our nation. We have also been victims of injustice, indifference, and cruelty, just as we ourselves have been authors of injustice, indifference, and cruelty.

Let us not be concerned with the nursing of old wounds, old fears, and old hatreds, but instead remember all we have done and what has been done to us, that we may know the greatness and the meanness of which we are each capable. Let us remember so that we can understand that it is each of us who must break the circle of retribution, that we may avoid becoming the victims of ourselves and come to live with those near to us and far from us in peace and justice, and on one great day, in love.

⤙

Our lives and surroundings are of intense importance to us, but we know that we exist as an infinitesimal dot in a vast universe which appears to offer no meaning nor purpose comprehensible to us, except what we ourselves create. In our myths and beliefs we have too much made ourselves the center of attention, as though we still believed we and our earth were the center of the universe. Let us look beyond our little world and contemplate the vastness of all that is created. May we then return to our little world, chastened and awed, to help make it—limited though it and we may be—as just and holy a place as we are able.

—⌣—

We can be supreme in the integrity of our own persons only if we have true humility. (By humility I do not mean self-hate or thinking ourselves of no value.) Only the humble person is secure in himself or herself, for the person who would act to save himself or herself or the image of oneself in the eyes of others is subject to the vagaries of chance and all the powers of the world outside that person. One whose self-esteem depends upon wealth or power is subject to every power and person who can affect that wealth and influence. The only secure person, the only person who lives on his or her own authority, is the person who has nothing to save— the person of humility. If I can have the humility to be nothing but what I am, then I have all the strength of my own character.

—⌣—

It is hard for us to face much that happens to us, and hardest of all is our coming to face our own shortcomings, our actions and inactions, our apathy and our uncaring. Let us seek not to escape to live in a world of past happiness nor in a fantasized future of perfection and personal satisfaction. Rather, may we seek to live in the imperfect present: to see ourselves and the world around us in our beauty and our ugliness, in our nobility and our falling short. It is in the world of this moment that we are able to give and receive love, in this moment that we are able to do acts of justice and charity, only in this and in each present moment that we can know beauty and know that we are at home in the world.

—⌣—

We are each capable of great nobility, of forming high ideals, and of serving those ideals; also, we are each imperfect, erring, and self-serving. The curious thing is that our nobility and our awareness of our imperfections go hand in hand: neither exists without the other. Only someone who cares can have a troubled conscience.

Each of us has known times of alienation from ourselves and from others, when we have lost our humility. Each of us has felt that sense of rebirth when we have found our lost selves by seeing ourselves as we are, in our imperfections. For the reminder of the power of rebirth through humility, I am grateful for the retelling of the birth in the manger.

We are not perfected creatures, with infinite wisdom, pure compassion, or unlimited strength of body and mind. Though we lack power to do all we would do, and though we often act in ways that are self-centered and uncaring, we also know that we have been given the strength and the means to seek out and acknowledge our self-deceptions, evasions, and the realities of our own lives. We know that there is a power that is within us and which can come through us to begin to heal our broken lives and our broken world. May we look within for that power, and will to use the gifts which have been given to us. Let us be givers of what we ourselves have been given.

Although we seek the best in ourselves and try to be instruments of good for others, we are constantly diverted by our needs, especially our need to think well of ourselves. May we not be concerned to be a helper, but rather to help; let us not aspire to be good, but rather to do good. May we seek not to be a lover, but to love. So, in losing ourselves, we may gain the whole world.

---

the failure
of success

We are the living expression of a body of humanity that goes back far into the past. Each generation has struggled to bring meaning to the lives of its members, and the task of each of us is to begin where they left off in the pursuit of truth and justice. The success of our lives is not measured by the status we have attained nor the wealth we have accumulated, but by how we have used the gifts we have received, great or small, in living lives of integrity and service.

It is troubling to encounter someone who is superior to us in any talent, ability, or capacity we like to believe we possess. But if we are to elevate ourselves and our society, we need to go beyond those feelings of competitiveness and envy, not to belittle superior talent or achievement to bring it down to our level, but to use the example of that person to inspire us to do better with what we have within ourselves.

We live in a world of a multiple hierarchy of talents and apti-
tudes: some people are endowed with many special talents; some
have one special aptitude; and most of us have whatever we have
in more modest measure. Every day we are confronted with that
inequality, and whether we proceed from that point to lead a
constructive life depends in some measure on how we respond to
the inequalities of life.

We can meet the challenge of inequality by changing our understanding of what it means to be a human being. As human beings
we are not competing in some cosmic contest to see who is worth
the most. That way leads to a constant state of insecurity when we
succeed, since we are always subject to being bested by a new com-
petitor, or to envy, resentment, and self-hatred when we do not
succeed.

Rather, to be human means to be a member of the human race
itself, part of a total organism in which we have a part to play
according to our capacities, to make our human race and our
world better than it would be without our participation. The
worth of our lives is not in whether we have been the equivalent of
a Jesus, a Gandhi, a Margaret Mead, or an Einstein, but whether
we have developed and used the talents and gifts of the body,
mind, and spirit which came to us with the gift of life.

Each of us has been frustrated by what we can look back and see
were bad decisions we have made, or misfortunes of chance, or the
result of what others have done or have failed to do, but there is no
value or solace in burying ourselves in a grief for what we might
have become. We must face what we are today, what talents and
capacities we have, and how we can realistically develop and use
those capacities in a world that is often not hospitable, but which
does give us opportunities for their use.

Become who you can be—great or average, genius or modest contributor to the life of the world. That is enough challenge for each of us, enough to make our lives worth living, enough to leave the world a better place than we found it. Become who you can be from this day forward.

~

Let us rejoice when we are successful in living in accord with our ideals, and on those occasions when we fail to live up to those ideals, let us seek to change our ways and set forth again, bowing neither to self-hate nor despair nor cynicism, burdened not with what we have done or left undone, but inspired by what we might now do.

~

We live in a country that has made a cult of success; we have a fascination with success and an aversion to failure. For many of us failure means *error,* but no one escapes the taste of failure. Complete success in life is a myth. The playing of the viola is like the unfolding performance of our own life itself: a constant falling short, a constant accommodation and adaptation, our letting the past be past, and our refocus upon the present moment, the only moment when life occurs.

It is not demanded of us that we be a success. All we must do is to take the leap of faith each day, to do as well as we can, this day. We will play our song of life out of tune; we will adjust and play again—still a little out of tune perhaps, but well enough to make our song. The bad notes we played yesterday are gone. The mistakes of tomorrow cannot be avoided by anticipation. This day is the day for our song, now, with joy, with faith.

~

In each of our lives we touch the sacred, the true, the beautiful, only when we lose our sense of separation from the whole, when we no longer think about being successful, powerful, clever, creative, respected, or even loved, when we become anonymous to ourselves.

This possibility for us to lose the sense of our own person in a larger sacred whole is not only for the great artists and scientists, but is available to each person. If we are to save our lives, we must lose ourselves in a life larger than our own.

~

It is not the fact of failure itself that is unbearable for many. What is most defeating is the fact of failure combined with our own belief that the failure shows that we ourselves are of little worth as persons. The issue is not factual failure, but our sense of personal failure.

The person who perseveres does so because he or she believes in what he or she is doing, believes that the hanging-on and the personal sacrifices are worth it, and—believing in what is being maintained in adversity—sees that he or she is of value in being part of the larger value served. Then even failure can be a success. On the other hand, the person who is defeated by failure is one who cannot accept the value of his or her own life and receives failure as a message or a reaffirmation that he or she is of little value. Unless we believe to some degree in the value of what we are spending the time and energy of our lives upon, any achievement we may attain will not satisfy us, and our triumphs will be hollow.

When we see on the one hand many persons who persevere through failure after failure, and on the other hand, many who seem to be defeated by relatively minor vicissitudes or for whom any success seems to be hollow, we can see certain differences of personality or character which appear to affect how we handle success and failure.

First, to be able to handle failures and successes we have to believe in our hearts that we are good for something; we have to believe in ourselves. If we do not believe in our basic value as a person, then all our actions and aspirations are already doomed to futility. No success will ever satisfy us, because whatever successes we have we shall attribute to causes outside ourselves: that we have been merely lucky, or had someone who really did it for us, or that if they really knew me, they wouldn't have promoted me, or whatever. We have to believe in ourselves.

There is also a phenomenon (much more widespread than generally realized) which is called "the fear of success," which can operate if we do not truly believe in ourselves. Without faith in ourselves, we shall be unable to handle both our successes and our failures, and we may program ourselves to fail as well.

If we find ourselves in this situation of having little faith in ourselves, that is where we must begin. One of the great characteristics of the human race is that we have the capacity within ourselves to change low self-esteem to self-acceptance and self-worth. We were not born with low self-esteem; if we have it, it is because we were cheated in our childhood or youth of our sense of self-worth— cheated by our parents or teachers or someone else, or by religion, or by the conditioning of a sexist or racist society, or by some early conditioning not yet understood. That is being cheated out of our human birthright, and whatever did that conditioning to us lies in our past.

Today our low self-esteem lies only within our own minds, and it is within our power to change. For some the nature of that conditioning is so deeply hidden or so deeply ingrained that we may need to get the help of psychotherapy to bring it to light and root it out. For many it can be done through the exercise of will and courage. But you can do it—if you want to do it.

We must have, however, what Robert Coles called a "compelling moral imperative." In his study of "the privileged ones" Dr. Coles found that the greatest lack among those who were unhappy was the absence of any personal sense of a moral imperative "except the imperative to stay where one is, hold onto what one has, add to the money and things already acquired."

Another way of saying this is that if we are to succeed in a real sense—if we are to be able to appreciate any success we do achieve—we must have a sense that our life is in some way serving a value higher than our own satisfaction. Pure self-satisfaction is not satisfying, so we need to choose some value or values to serve, and to aim higher than ourselves, and higher than something we can achieve completely. If our goal has been modest and it has been achieved and the value realized, then we need a new goal. Our pursuit of whatever worthy value we choose to help realize is indeed one of the best ways to give us a sense of self-worth. We are devoting our lives, at least in part, to something that is more important than ourselves, and so we partake of the value we pursue. We create our own worth by what we choose as our goals.

It is one of the ironies of human existence that human beings can even get a sense of self-worth when they pursue unworthy goals which let them feel part of something larger than themselves. Nazism was attractive to many Germans because it brought a sense of worth to a people who had lost confidence in themselves because of their military, economic, and political failures. Our task is to choose goals which are worthy of our lives: the love and welfare of our family, the justice of our nation, the peace of our planet—and alongside those, more modest goals of success in our daily work.

Our achievements are made worthy because they move us toward something beyond ourselves, even though they fail to give us a complete achievement of those values. Let us not be so much concerned then with what may bring us success, but with what may be worthwhile for us to do. That may not be the way of dramatic success, but it can be the way we muddle through a life worth living.

~

One of the deep maladies of our country is that success is thought to be the equivalent of happiness, but those things that can be achieved are ephemeral, and the highest goals to which we aspire we shall never attain. The higher we aim, the more we miss the mark. There is no flower nor human being without flaw, but each rose and each man and woman is holy in each moment of existence. We are what we are. There is nothing in us to save; we have never been lost. We have only failed to see that we are safe and whole.

~

Remember that it is those who are elevated by the highest who know most deeply their falling short, that the price of a caring heart is the pain of compassion, and that the more intense our sense of life, the greater the act of faith required of us to engage that life. What is required of us is not to succeed, but to act now and here, as well as we can, in faith and trust. So may we be a friend to others and to ourselves in time of disappointment and despair, and love the world and all its gifts to us.

~

A question may form slowly in our minds: "Is what I am doing in the service of my company worthy of me as a human being? Is it worth the pouring out of my life's energy?" It is good that we come to ask ourselves that from time to time. It is the kind of question that arises no matter what we do or where we work, even when we live lives of relative happiness. It is a disturbing question, but we know that we need to disturb ourselves occasionally, or our moral faculties will atrophy.

～

The goal is work, but not too much, and idleness, but not too much. Work is at the center of a worthwhile life, and the cessation of work is not a goal for us to try to attain. Serenity is in our involvement in our projects, projects which will change as the stages of our life change. To work is to celebrate life. Let it be said of us that we were workers in this world, that we were celebrators of Creation, that we were co-creators, and then when we depart from it, that we have left this world a little better for our having been here.

～

the message
of anger

To be human means to have impulses of emotion (anger, fear, sexuality, and so forth) that may violate our own moral standards, but the real issue is how we deal with those impulses and emotions, how we learn to accept them for what they are, and go on to live as responsibly and as compassionately as we can.

⤙

We need to keep anger from destroying our personal lives and the lives of those we love. We can understand our own anger as a message to us from our inner selves, and we can understand anger in others as a message to us of their fears and needs.

One major cause of our anger is our belief that our image of ourselves is being attacked, criticized, or put down. Our self-image is our image of what we would like to think we are. When that is threatened, we respond with anger—especially when we are not so sure that we are really as good or noble as we would like to think we are. In contrast with the anger caused by an attack on our self-image, there is the anger which we feel when our integrity, self-sufficiency, freedom, health, or well-being is *in fact* threatened. Our response needs to be quite different if our anger is caused by an attack on our self-image from what it should be if the threat is to our real selves.

It is not quietism that is needed, but the raising in our churches and synagogues of the great social and human needs of our time as spiritual (or religious) issues. What is needed is a greater sense that all human beings on the earth are one people and that each of us is part of that great human family. We need the perception that when any human being on the earth suffers, part of us suffers and is threatened. What is needed then is *more* anger at the real injustice in this world and a collective response on our part to that anger.

This meeting house must be more than a house of worship and celebration. It must also be a house of anger, anger that is kindled by the recollection that there are many whose lives are still stifled by poverty and injustice, anger that leads us out these doors to action. We shall not have simply comfortable middle-class rites and liturgies here and fall under the condemnation of the great prophet Amos, who attacked the religion of his time for its passive celebrations while the world burned.

We must accept our anger at injustice and not be consumed by it; we must direct that anger not at persons who may be the instruments of injustice, but at the injustices themselves. We must look not for scapegoats, but for help and alleviation of suffering.

Anger of a self-serving kind is the cause of much strife and war, but anger at an unjust world and at a scheme of things in which the lives of children and adults are stunted or diminished while we have the means to attack those evils and reduce them—that anger can be a force for good. That anger is the anger of the great prophets of religion, and among enough of us, it may lead to action and to a better world.

If we are angry enough to work for a world of peace and health and justice, then we may one day come to a world when we shall have cause to be angry no longer. Until that day comes, let us have a loving anger.

~

We are human, and we wish to come to terms with our humanity. Because we are human, there are times when we are angry with those closest to us. May we have the courage to face the reality of our anger, so that we may understand it and control its exercise.

Because our friends and those dear to us are human, there are times when they will be angry at us. May we hear their anger, and beneath it the message of their needs and fears. May we forgive others, that they may forgive us more easily, and finally, may we forgive ourselves, that we may be free to live a life of compassion.

~

Anger long indulged will consume the angry person and cut him or her off from the world and from fellow human beings, whether that anger be against others or against oneself.

Anger is a message. There is a meaning in our anger or in the anger of others, and our work is to search out that meaning and that message. When I feel anger in myself, there is no point in denying its reality to myself, so I let myself experience it, which is not the same thing as expressing it or acting on it. I simply let myself experience my feeling of anger, and then try to discover what I am telling myself. What is threatening me? Is someone trying to take advantage of me, or manipulate me? How realistic are these perceptions of mine? Is some unrealistic self-image of mine being threatened? These are the questions we need to ask ourselves when we become angry.

When we see another person's anger, we do them the greatest
service and treat them as full human beings if we are willing to
recognize that they are angry and to ask ourselves what the message
is in their anger. Their anger can tell us their needs, for it is based
upon their perception that they are being injured or threatened in
some way. Do they feel rejected or exploited? Is there some way
we can support them or confirm them?

In most cases in our daily lives we can learn much about what
we need to do with ourselves and about what others' needs are, if
we listen for anger and try to respond in a caring way when we
discover it. If we listen hard enough for the message when we hear
anger, we may even forget to be angry ourselves.

～

Anger is our response to a situation in which we see ourselves—
or someone or something we value—threatened or disvalued. This
gives us an important clue to understanding anger in others or in
ourselves. The key question to ask in the presence of anger is,
"What is it that this angry person values that he or she feels is
being threatened or put down?"

We need to avoid having our anger consume us and render us
impotent. Our energy must be used to heal, not to punish, so we
must transform our anger into a force which does not feed our
hatred. We must understand the dark side of our soul and bring
it to light. We need to become aware of our doubts, weaknesses,
fears, all that threatens to diminish us. When we no longer have to
hide from what we do not like within ourselves or to pretend that
we are stronger or wiser or more secure than we are, then we are
free from the vice of the anger which we use to support our
pretenses.

～

To be forgiving does not mean that we do not get angry, or that we do not defend ourselves. To be forgiving does not mean that we make ourselves an emotional pin cushion or a doormat for another.

We can learn from the practice of forgiveness that it is possible to survive injustice, hurt, and rejection without becoming the victim of our own vindictiveness. It is possible to respond with anger at injustice, to act for justice, and to defend ourselves and others, all without vindictiveness, but all with the presence of forgiveness.

Between two people who love one another the understanding and practice of forgiveness means that I must be concerned not to prove that I am right and you are wrong, or that you must suffer for something you have done, but to let you know how I and our relationship are being hurt. Through our understanding of one another we can resolve our problems for the health and integrity of each of us alone and, if it can be worked out, together.

﹌

May we recognize within ourselves the natural feelings of anger and fear, desire and yearning, pleasure and pain, joy and grief, and come to accept those feelings as truly part of ourselves, not seeking to transfer them to gods or devils outside ourselves.

Let us accept not only these feelings but also our responsibility to transform them—good and bad—into acts of caring for others and for our own selves. So may we use the gift of our own life to heal our own selves and others rather than to hurt, and to give more than we have received.

﹌

guilt, a universal human experience?

We must acknowledge to ourselves when we have done something we should not have done, or failed to do what we should have done. If we deny to ourselves that we have violated our personal standards of right and wrong, then we deny the reality of who we are. If we insist that we are someone we are not, someone who is without fault, we deny our own real nature. I don't believe in wallowing in guilt, but I don't know any other way to health than to acknowledge mistakes, know sadness and the feeling of being sorry, and then proceed. We can know that we have erred and can turn again.

As we sense an urge within us to conduct our lives by a morality that is higher than we are ever able to achieve, we rejoice in the gift of that moral urge. When we falter or fail to live up to that high inner standard of moral conduct, we know guilt and remorse. May that guilt and remorse not be a burden unresolved which weighs down our daily lives; rather, let us transform that grief into new life, into resolution and conduct which leads us to the best that is within us. May we forgive ourselves in order to pass beyond the burdens of our guilt and vanity, to be of service to others and honor the good that remains in us.

～

I believe in the capacity of the human heart and mind to find what is real and what is true, if we will to do so and if we apply ourselves to the task. We have each been granted the full gift of life, to be able to know and understand the world as it is and our own place in it. With all its contradictions the world waits for each of us to embrace it in its fullness. We live in the real world—with imperfect choices and the guilt those choices bring—and in our search for goodness and truth in our lives, we can be messengers of a spirit that can only come to birth through each of us.

～

Feelings of guilt are part of almost all of our lives. If we are healthy human beings, we would not want to live a life that knows no guilt. There are two kinds of guilt which we experience. The first is our guilt at having violated our inner sense of morality. Even if there *is* good in us, we *have* done things which we ought not to have done, and we *have* left undone what we ought to have done. We have sometimes been unfaithful to what we in our hearts know is good or true. No denial or avoidance will take away that guilt.

Instead, what is required of us is that we accept ourselves as guilty, but not wallow in some self-punishment that never heals us and only makes us suffer and suffer. The goal is not to be pure and clean, but to accept ourselves as we are, without the vanity of self-pity or self-loathing, and to live today and tomorrow in the light of today and tomorrow and not in the shadow of yesterday. Yes, we do injure ourselves by our moral failures, but we need to walk with imperfect steps, with imperfect minds and hearts, with wounds imperfectly healed, rather than to pick at our wounds of guilt or to live in the fantasy that we will be restored to the innocence of infancy.

We fail ourselves and others, but let us make restoration where restoration is possible, heal where there can be healing, mend our torn selves, and go on our way in our mended state. There are new trials, new opportunities, new occasions for us to do the good that is within us.

A second kind of guilty experience is what I call *the guilt of being alive:* a guilt we feel because we are involved in others' lives and in our own, and we are not omnipotently able to prevent hurt or failure. We are in the bind of feeling that we have power but not enough power—a kind of survivor's guilt.

Guilt is an almost universal human experience. We handle our guilt not by denying it or trying to be psychoanalyzed out of it, but by acknowledging it and accepting it, by taking it upon ourselves honestly. We must not try to get rid of guilty feelings, even though we are beset by religions and philosophies which offer to do that for us. All medicines for guilt will drug the most human part in each of us, but by accepting and acknowledging our guilt to our deepest selves, we become open to forgiving ourselves; we become reconciled with our deepest selves; we become whole again.

The essence of the Puritan conscience is that in the back of our minds there is a quiet but persistent voice that keeps saying to us, "Don't waste your life. Don't waste your time or your energy on unworthy pursuits. Avoid the trivial. Devote your precious life to important things."

The good side to having such a Puritan conscience is that in the practical and political world our sense of unease drives us to do things worth doing and to work for causes that we would otherwise prefer to avoid. However, there is a disadvantage to prodding ourselves too hard or unremittingly, for we need space in our lives around those worthy activities: we can have too many worthy activities, too many valuable things going on, too many interesting people. If we are modern Puritans, we clutter our lives not with the trivial, but with the important.

～

When we are disappointed that we have not attained our aspirations, may we forego blame, either of ourselves or of others. Instead, let us look again at the real world, at the truth in which we live, and make new dreams that seek again a better and higher way. So may our dreams be not our tormentors, but our guides and our inspiration.

～

the spirit of gratitude

Each of us passes through times when we are fragmented and at odds with the best in ourselves, but we also know times when we feel the health and love that is within each of us. For our faith in the return of hope and in the power of love over apathy and despair, we give thanks. We are thankful too for the miracle of our consciousness of life and its necessary companion, our consciousness of death.

It is when we no longer take our lives and our pleasures for granted that we know how to be truly grateful. One of the greatest joys is to be filled with gratitude for the gift of our lives, and the greatest obstacle to being able to give such thanks is *not* the presence of adversity, but the absence of humility. Only a humble person knows how to be thankful.

Let us offer thanksgiving without looking over our shoulder
at others; may we look with humility and gratitude at the greatness of the Creation of which we are part and have a thanksgiving
not of comparison, but of joyful acceptance.

～

We offer thanks,
- for the eyes we have been given, with which we behold
  the beauty of nature and the vastness of the universe;
- for the ears we have been given, through which we hear
  poetry and music singing of the Soul which includes all
  our little souls;
- for the heart we have been given, which stirs us to understanding and compassion;
- for the mind we have been granted which, in giving us
  the burden of knowledge of our own mortality, also
  makes us aware of that which is beyond time and death.

～

The spirit of thanksgiving is at the heart of true religiousness.
To be thankful means to have an open, full heart, and to say to life
and God or what one may even believe to be an indifferent universe: "I am filled with gratefulness for the gift of life I have, for
the presence of my home, my friends and family, and for the world
beyond me with its goodness and fruitfulness."

In order to get in touch with our feelings of thankfulness, we
have to be in touch with all our feelings, and if we are unable or
unwilling to get in touch with all our feelings—good and bad,
happy and not happy—then we miss feeling thankful too.

We are grateful for our homes, our freedom, our opportunity to work for a world of peace and justice, our power to live each day as it may come, and our power to find renewal after defeat, strength after loss, and rebirth after spiritual death.

—

We are thankful for the gift of consciousness, although it is a difficult gift to bear. It reminds us of both our conscious and unconscious errors; it tells us we have left undone those things which we ought to have done and we have done those things we ought not to have done. It tells us that there is a darkness and a falling-short within us.

We give thanks for this mirror of ourselves which reflects an image we do not always want to see. We are also aware that there is health in us, and that our discontent with ourselves may be a divine discontent that will lead us to struggle with the darkness with all the power of the health in us. For that health, for that power, for that discontent which invites us to a more noble life, we are grateful.

—

We are the product of everyone we have ever known. We have learned what is goodness from seeing goodness in others, just as we have learned the meaning of evil from the example and presence of evil in others. We have been taught to love only by those who have themselves known how to love. For all who have taught us what it means to be human, for those who have shown us by their own lives the way we ourselves choose to follow, and for the spirit which makes all human life, good-ness, and love possible, we are filled with gratitude.

—

Let us be thankful for our awareness that even our powers of conscience and our passion for justice can be used in uncaring and hurtful ways. We are glad that we are enabled to see how even our urge to be good and to do good can be mixed with less worthy goals. We have been given the gift to see that beneath all good and evil there is a power which animates all things and that we are part of one great unity in which we live and move and have our being. For these gifts we give thanks.

choice:
the power
to act
and change

We are responsible. We are capable of change, and the beginning of responsibility and of change is to say that if there is a Devil, it is one we have been nurturing and protecting within our own minds. We are each a human being, capable of great nobility and great depravity, and free to choose.

～

Most of us are trapped in a web of condition or circumstance, and we must come to terms with those conditions and shape our lives within narrower limits than we would choose. Whatever our condition, we have power to make ours a life of worth and dignity. We temporize, we make excuses for avoiding change: we tell our

selves we are too young or too old, that it is too early or too late in
our lives to act, that a project is too novel to attempt or a habit too
ingrained to stop. We excuse ourselves and retreat from the field.
Whatever our limitations, let us face the choices that lie open
before us. May any fear of change we possess be exceeded by a
greater concern that when we come to die, we shall not have lived.

～

A concern that we make our life healthy, worthy, and noble in
its aims and accomplishments is not narcissism, but a respect for
the sacredness of creation itself. Self-concern then becomes a
religious concern.

I extend an appeal to the will, for it is only by an act of the will
that we act in our own lives out of religious self-concern. If we
wish to have others love us, let us begin by loving others, by draw-
ing a caring circle around those persons and causes beyond ourselves. Let our care for our neighbor come not because of what we
expect our neighbor can do for us or how good he or she can make
us feel. Rather, let our care proceed from our perception of our
common humanity.

Remember that when we are sick, the world is not sick, and that
our own death is not the death of the universe. When we can see
and feel in the heart of our being that we are part of a universal soul
that was here before we were born and will continue long after the
last human being has passed from life, then we shall have the means
not to escape pain and loss, but to bear them, and then we shall
ourselves be able to live as a manifestation of that universal soul.

～

If we wish to live moral lives, we must have courage: courage to see things as they truly are, courage to see the likely consequences of our action and inaction, and courage to do what needs to be done, despite pain to ourselves and to others. Moral courage is required of us in our daily lives, and it is our choice: we are capable of knowing good from evil, justice from injustice, truth from falsity. Every day we are called to choose goodness and justice and truth, in hope and in fear, in happiness and in pain.

⌁

Resistance to change may be more subtle than simple fear of injury or economic loss. Often it is fear of some loss that may proceed from disruption of a complicated kind of equilibrium we have attained in our relationships with other people. Most of us (after long periods of adjustment) have worked out a social mechanism with one another; with our friends, co-workers, and family we have developed a complicated signal system to minimize friction and keep the social machine running. It may not be a perfect adjustment (the machine may creak and groan once in a while), but it eventually smoothes out. If I change much, I am going to throw the whole mechanism out of adjustment, which will mean that I will have to deal with a whole set of new decisions and unknowns. There may be changes in my living conditions and my relationship and personal goals. That is going to take a lot of energy I may not want to spend.

For the same reasons that we resist change in ourselves, we resist change in others, and others resist it in us. A change in any member in a network of relationships means that the other members will have to accommodate to that change—in other words, they too will have to change to some degree. But perhaps we have reached a point of discomfort or dissatisfaction in our lives, so that we decide we need to change. This will mean either a change externally (such as in a job or a relationship) or a change internally (in our attitudes, values, or goals). What then?

Then we get to the heart of the matter: whether you change or not depends entirely upon you. If there is a God out there of any kind, even a God whose eye is upon the sparrow, that God is not going to come in and change your life for you while you passively enjoy the passing scene. You are going to have to be at least a full co-creator in your change. If there is *not* a God out there, then you will have to be the sole initiator and creator of whatever change you go through. Either way, it is a matter of your willing and your doing. I do no one a favor if I feed a fantasy that change can occur unless you *will* it and *do* it. We learn to swim by getting in the water; we never learn to swim by thinking about the water, or by trying to figure out some way to swim without getting wet.

I have never found a way to do anything except to do it. I have never found a way to write a sermon, except to sit down in front of the typewriter and begin to type. The only way to make a decision is to do it. I do not mean that we should decide out of impulse or desperation—quite the contrary. I mean that, after we have thought about it and struggled with it and weighed the pros and cons and listened to our intuition and perhaps sought advice, after all that, we *do* it.

I am appealing to the absolute primacy of your will as the agency of your change, but I am not making a naïve appeal to your will. There are social, economic, psychological, and perhaps physical factors which create resistance in all of us to change. We have to deal with those factors as best we can, and try to change them for ourselves and for others in order to make change more likely or easier. But after all has been thought and intellectualized and wrestled with, we always come to the point where it is simply a matter of *will*.

The exercise of our wills can be a religious act, for it is the point at which we accept our role as a creator of our own lives. The great religious traditions in history have always put the exercise of will at the center of religious life. Any religion worthy of the name calls us to make decisions about our lives, decisions that will change our lives and which may run against the current of our culture and our social conditioning.

In the less visible arena of private life and hidden personal decisions, it is our religious traditions which take the lead in rejecting counsels of despair or apathy, and which tell us that we do have the power of decision over the quality of our lives and the power to affect the lives of those around us. The question is not whether we have the power for change and reconciliation. The question is whether we will use that power to save ourselves, in this life, for this life.

~

In times of doubt we seek the security of the familiar and habitual. We fear change, even though it may be change for the better. We prefer the smooth way and the level path. May we seek the strength of spirit to face what we know we need to do and to have the confidence that life lies before us and not behind us, no matter how long or short our future may be. Let us move to a deeper experience of life, knowing that those who wish to save their lives shall lose them, and that the greatest risk is to risk nothing.

~

A transforming religion is a way of living in which we open ourselves to change and growth, even though that way may be difficult or painful. A transforming religion is one in which we as individuals go through transformation into new persons. It asks that we open ourselves to life, whatever that may bring, rather than live by trying to hang on to what we can.

Such a religion demands that we pursue that quality within each of us which tells us what we need to believe or do in order to be truly ourselves and to be real persons. There is a divine quality or presence within each of us which is there waiting for us, if we will open to it; there is some sense of the absolute within us which we must pursue in order to be authentic. Our pursuit of authenticity and of a religion of transformation may lead us for a while through times of emotional insecurity, but we want more than comfort, security, and an easy religion. Unless we turn and become like little children, we shall not be in touch with the most inner part of ourselves that reveals what we must do to grow and be transformed throughout our lives.

～

Let us have our discussions, but then we must each make our commitments and decisions, based upon the values and beliefs we have accepted according to our own authority. You can always change your mind, your beliefs, and your values, but start somewhere, whether you decide to be a Christian or non-Christian, theist or non-theist, pantheist, panentheist, or whatever.

I did not come to this church to make it a comfortable fence for theological mugwumps. Yes, render to Caesar what is Caesar's and to God what is God's, and you had better decide for yourself what is Caesar's and what is God's. The authority to know the truth and to know how to do the truth is within each one of you. Neither your mother nor your father nor I nor anyone can give you that authority: you already have it, if you are able to take it with the full responsibility it carries.

～

We invoke the spirit of reformation, remembering the great reformers of history, who made the world for a time a less orderly, less comfortable place, in order that it might become a more just and honest place. We invoke within ourselves the spirit of personal reform, that we may be less comfortable with our old selves in order to find new selves of greater depth and honesty.

In our reform—personal, political, and religious—let us avoid the temptation to hate the objects of our reform. May we act from love, not hate, and seek the larger, not the smaller, truth; let us pursue higher ideals rather than scapegoats. Let our reform be directed at the present for the sake of the future and not be consumed in blame for the past. So may we be enlarged and not diminished by our reformation, and others be our beneficiaries and not our victims.

～

Our reform is never over. If there is the Divine in us, it must be in the urge we have to grow, to push out our personal boundaries, to encompass more and more, to open more to the world of divergent values and beliefs, and to find a way of acting and participating in our growing world.

The issue is this: will we move toward simply defending what we have and are, will we defend the shrinking perimeter of our self and become a fortress under constant siege, while the self we defend grows smaller and smaller, as we devote more and more energy to preserve less and less? Or will we move toward a greater acceptance of the world, toward expanding the boundaries of our self, toward growth, toward recognizing our urge to grow? Will our life be one in which we grow and expand until at our death we have learned to realize that we are one with all there is, or will our life be one in which we die in a shrunken, tiny, isolated, spiritual and emotional cell, prisoners of the fears and ideologies of a time long gone by? Will we be reformers or victims of failure to reform?

～

As our lives spin out from year to year, we become ensnared in the patterns of the personality we have constructed, and trapped in the images of ourselves in the eyes of those around us. We are timid to challenge those patterns and to disappoint the expectations of others. We prefer the expected with its dissatisfactions to a more promising but uncertain unknown.

Nevertheless, we feel within ourselves the urge to develop, to grow, to re-form, to live a life that we have the potential and the power to live. May we listen to that still small voice within us which summons us to the present rather than to the past, which calls us to shed our constricting shell for the larger life.

~

What does it mean to be a victim? In popular usage we call someone a victim who is hurt by an accident or disease or at the hands of another, but I am not referring to that popular sense of what it means to be a victim. All of us at some time suffer or are hurt; all of us ultimately succumb to our mortality, but we are not all victimized by life. Some seem to bear adversity, pain, and death in a way that makes their lives a triumph, while others are destroyed or made living shells by similar events. Some become victims, and some do not.

The only person who can victimize us is our self. We can, of course, every day be injured or even killed. We suffer pain, separation, death, despair, loneliness; we hurt and are hurt. We suffer from our actions and inactions. We live in a real world. Yet, whether we become a victim of life does not depend upon what happens to us, but upon how we respond to what happens to us.

There is a power in us and available to us that makes each of us able to bear anything that is meted out to us. None of us need be a victim. Yet, many of us are victims. Life constantly tempts us to become victims, to accept victimization, to victimize ourselves. We are constantly tempted to avoid the reality about ourselves and the world in which we live. We are tempted to believe that we are better than we are, less vulnerable than we are. We are tempted to believe that the world is not indifferent to us and our hopes.

The process by which we can avoid making ourselves victims, the process by which we come again to live in the real world and avoid the temptation of trying to escape that reality, that process we call grieving. Grief is ordinarily thought of as the process we go through when someone close to us dies. That is one kind of grief, but there are many other kinds, for grief is the very common and vital process of our coming to accept and adapt to anything unhappy which has happened to us.

Grief is the process by which we make real what first seems unreal: yes, he or she is really dead; yes, my life as bound up with him or her is truly over, and I am in a different life now; yes, my feelings of being abandoned and perhaps of anger are real. In many other situations we have grief: yes, my marriage has failed, it is really over; yes, I have failed in my work or my career; yes (in other words), I am a vulnerable, hurt, and mortal human being, and I must begin to live in the truth from where I am this present moment. That process of grieving over the loss of what we have cherished—whether that has been a person, a goal, or a self-image—that process may take considerable time, but if we do not go through it, we become a victim.

If, after the shock of our loss, we are able to go through the process of grief, we become able to see ourselves as we really are, changed and diminished. We cannot be a victim if we see ourselves and accept ourselves as we truly are. It is only then that we can affirm life fully and not become a prey to our own self-esteem.

Only when we insist on hanging on to our innocence or to our illusions about ourselves do we become victims, only then do we give away our power to be healed. If you must believe you are innocent of anger or of pride, envy, hatred, greed, or jealousy, you give power over your own life to anyone or anything that will reveal any of your imperfections. If you have to believe you are innocent of any moral lapse, you make yourself a victim when you make any human error. If you have to be a successful parent, you give to your children the power to make you a victim of your own illusions, since they then have the power to make you fail in your own eyes. If you have to be right in every argument with your spouse or friend, you give them the power to threaten your sense of self on every occasion in which you disagree.

To refuse to be a victim of our illusions and demand for innocence means to be free. We become free from the restrictions and the imprisonment of what we hope others will think of us, free of our *image*. We become free from the imprisonment of our illusions about what we would like to think we are, free from having to defend ourselves when we sense those illusions are threatened.

If I lose my money in business or bad investments, I may be poor, but I am not ruined. If I am betrayed by someone I love, then I am hurt, but not destroyed. If I suffer from being falsely accused or from gossip, I have been wounded, but I will survive. If I lose someone I love, I may know pain, separation, and loss, but I can come back after my grief has subsided to live as a vital human being. If I have myself been the cause of unnecessary suffering for others, if I have hurt others, if I have done wrong, then I can begin on the path back to health by acknowledging to myself that I have done wrong and that I am capable of wrong now.

We are only ruined or destroyed by our self-judgment when our image of ourselves requires us to be rich, successful, healthy, or without fault or loss. That is what is meant when we hear, "Whosoever shall seek to save his life shall lose it, and whosoever shall lose his life shall preserve it." [Luke 17:33] Many religions understand that such a process of coming to terms with our real and imperfect selves is necessary to our becoming whole. The

word *atonement* (at-one-ment) means the process by which we
restore ourselves by this confrontation with our imperfect selves.
From his prison cell, Oscar Wilde wrote:

> When first I was put into prison some people advised me
> to try to forget who I was. It was ruinous advice. It is only
> by realizing what I am that I have found comfort of any
> kind. Now [upon my release] ... to try to forget that I have
> ever been in prison would mean that I would always be
> haunted by an intolerable sense of disgrace and that those
> things that are meant for me as much as for anybody
> else—the beauty of the sun and moon, the pageant of the
> seasons, the music of daybreak and the silence of great
> nights, the rain falling through leaves, or the dew creeping
> over the grass and making it silver—would all be tainted
> for me, and lose their healing power and their power of
> communicating joy. To regret one's own experience is to
> put a lie into the lips of one's own life. It is no less than a
> denial of the soul.
>
> *-De Profundis*

So, we have a choice, each of us: do we want to be a victim
of ourselves, to sacrifice ourselves on the altar of our self-illusions?
Or do we want to be free to live in the real world, fallible, imperfect,
mortal, and without innocence? Unlike any other creatures that
we know, we have been granted the power of self-consciousness.
We have been given the means to know that we each have the
power to act for good and for evil, to love and to be uncaring, to
act for justice and for injustice. It is our very power of consciousness
that tempts us to become victims in our search for innocence and
the illusion of perfection, but it is also that power which allows us
to accept the fullness of the gift of our lives, to live in our imperfect
and real world as instruments of love and justice, to say *yes* to life.

Though there is much we cannot change in the world as it presents itself to us, there is much we can change in ourselves in the way we respond to that world. Though we know the limitations of our power, we also know that we have the power to shape our own lives. May we have the courage to live life to its depths and heights, with the faith that when we are willing to confront its meanness and pain we shall come to know its joys and glories. So may we live what is life and learn what it has to teach while we are here to learn.

TAKING ON THE WORLD:

the risks
and demands
of meeting

The message of the great religions of the world is that all human beings are brothers and sisters—all of us are part of one family—and each of us must seek a way of life that honors each and all of us, despite our weaknesses and our failures.

❧

May we venture every day in the faith that whatever our condition we have the power to be a channel of love to those near to us. Let us nurture the hope in others and in ourselves that we each will be equal to the challenges of life, and may we act this day and every day with the power that we have been given to confirm one another in acts of mutual recognition and compassion. So may we give to others the bread of love that others have given to us.

❧

Each of us is a separate and sacred being, a being made most real when it weaves itself into the pattern of all Being. The harmony of all Being includes each of us within it, and its health requires our individual effort. So we live: each of us a needed part of the Universal Soul—each in all, and all in each, one pattern, one truth, one body.

～

When we give up our resentment and any claim to retribution, we become able to survive the injustice, hurt, and rejection we have suffered, without poisoning ourselves with our own vindictiveness. Most of us have known people who have diminished their lives because they could not forgive, who have carried their hurts on their backs as immense burdens until those burdens bore them down. Forgiveness is needed not to save the one who does wrong, but the one who receives wrong, the one who forgives.

How do we come to forgive another? We become able to forgive another when we can so identify ourselves with that other that we can say to ourselves: "I know enough about you—how you are and the reason you have come to be the way you are—that even though I may hate what you have done, I understand that if I had gone through what you have, I might have done just what you have done, or worse. I am fully capable of everything you have done."

Forgiving does not mean that we must accede to unjust demands, nor that we approve of what has been done. Forgiveness does not even mean that we must be reconciled with the one we forgive; that may be impossible through death or separation, or it may be self-destructive to become reconciled. But forgiving does mean that the forgiver is relieved of a great burden, and it means that conflict between forgiver and forgiven can be ended.

～

May we be just, but more than just, tempering our judgment with compassion. May we do what is right, but not blind ourselves to acts of cruelty and uncaring in a narrowness of vision and self-righteousness. We must treat others who err as we ourselves would be treated in our own errors, and our words and deeds must be made with the spirit of compassion, so that from our differences we can be reconciled into the strength of one caring community, remaining one in the spirit.

⤙

The less I am aware of my own self, the more I become aware of the joys and the sufferings of others. Compassionate feelings which do not bear fruit in compassionate acts are barren narcissism. Compassion which stops short of response is not true compassion.

⤙

We try to think of ways to be of more service to our fellow human beings. We must search our hearts to know the rationalizations and the self-deceptions which lead us to actions or inactions we like to believe are for the sake of others, when they may be for our own sake. Let us be guided by understanding care to act in ways which give the greatest dignity and respect to one another and to ourselves.

In our trials may we be fully present and not withholding from one another, so that we can strengthen each other by our compassionate presence as we walk through the darkest valleys; in our happy times may we be present to one another and share our rejoicing, so that others can know the joy of sharing our joy. Then we will be part of one another and our lives part of a larger life that came before us and will continue after us.

⤙

There are many who live quiet lives of principle, who march to their own drummer. They are the conscience and the spirit of our society, demanding truth and integrity not only from our leaders, but in their relationships with husbands, wives, and friends. If we would be their friends, they do not demand that we be perfect any more than they would claim to be perfect, but they would prefer an honest solitude to a dishonest companionship, and if we are fortunate enough to be their friend, they make us better than we would have been.

May we who have suffered past despair and disappointment share our renewed hope and our new revelation with others, so that this message of hope and promise can come to those now in the midst of despair and disappointment.

When we act in love, we do not feel as though we are having to exert an effort of our will to do the loving act. The genuine loving act proceeds as though by necessity from us when we give our attention to the person we love. What is required of us is our sight, that we look at the world as it is and the other person as he or she is. When we look, we see the other, and if we feel love for the other, we also feel how we can act for the other to realize her or his own worth. Then we proceed in sincerity, simplicity, and necessity to act in love. First, we see, then we love; finally, we act in love.

Too often our problem is not that we are unwilling to make the effort to do the loving thing, but that we are not willing to look, so that our love and our efforts are not stimulated. We do not look at the person who needs our words and actions; we refuse to see what they are showing us and to hear what they are telling us.

There are many times when we do not *want* to look at the real world or the real person. Indeed, it is not possible to lead a healthy, sane, and caring life if one looks too much and too long at the real neediness and misery in this world. We need our islands of fantasy and withdrawal and sleep and recovery, but there are limits on how long we can allow ourselves to sleep in the real world. Above all there is the danger that we shall deceive ourselves into believing that we are in love with this world—that is, in love with life—when all we want to do is to look at valentines.

Love does not proceed from pursuit of "love", but from being willing to enlarge one's being to include the being of another, from being willing to look at the other exactly as he or she is in the same way that we look at our own body and mind.

Beware of any religious leader who speaks in general of love, truth, compassion, and righteousness, but who would have us turn away from the real world. True religion is not a heavenly fantasy, but an affirmation of a real world of heaven and hell that lies before us. Let us be lovers of the real world.

Too often we have sought to be comforted, rather than to be aroused to the need for the comfort of others. Too often we have sought solace, rather than justice, and a quiet, rather than a compassionate, heart. Too often we have sought to be protected from reality, rather than to live in the truth. We have blamed the victims for their misery, and we have rejected the messengers of injustice for the inconvenience of their truths.

May our minds remain open to the truth, comforting or discomforting, and our hearts open to the sorrows as well as the joys of others. Let our hands remain at the task of healing and caring work, to the end.

If we are truly seekers, then we are willing to learn from others. If we are willing to learn from others, then we are willing to accept others from time to time as being our teachers, as having something to teach us. Of course at the last we must turn to our own inner authority, but should not that be after we have first been students ourselves?

~

As we open ourselves to the presence of the mystery of life and the power which surges about and within us, we become aware of one another—that we stand together before that mystery and that power. There are those of us who are grieving, who suffer, who must live with special anxieties of family or disease or difficulty. With them we share this presence and remind them that they are not alone. We seek to be renewed in our inner strength and to be instruments of the power of compassion, reconciliation, and caring response. So may we be open to receive the glory of life, in which each of us can play our passing part.

~

There is something we can give one another: we do not have to share the details of our private successes and failures, but we can share the awareness that we are not alone. We are each a pilgrim, and we can be in the company of other pilgrims who seek lives beyond the demands for conformity that surround us. We can abandon our preoccupation with success and failure, and instead cultivate and celebrate the eternal revelation of the heart which reveals to each of us what we can stake our lives upon as being the right thing, the just thing, the good thing, the caring thing to do, in each advancing moment.

~

From the diversity of religious traditions we understand that no story, no legend, no accumulated heritage will serve all of us in our diversity. We seek to know, understand, and be enlarged by the insights of various strands of religion, so that we come to understand that ways and forms which first appear strange to us come from our common human experience.

Then we will realize that all men and women on earth are our brothers and sisters, all on a common journey together. So may we not fear our diversity, but move toward mutual respect, reconciliation, peace, and the mutual enrichment of our lives.

~

A deep love relationship is one in which we have expanded the boundary of our own sense of self to include another person: their joys become our joys and their anxieties, our anxieties. Love in that sense is not infatuation or passion, in which we see the other as means to our own happiness or gratification, but we see the other as a person in her or his own right, at the same time that our own heart has enlarged to include theirs. In my experience I would say that this happens—if it happens—usually after marriage. A passionate love affair is not a love relationship in that sense.

On the other hand, there are many lives of great depth which are lived without the commitment of a love relationship, or without such a relationship much of the time. That may not always be easy, but it is not always easy to live in a love commitment either.

~

May our love for our own freedom be tempered by our love for the common good. Let our concern for the good of others be accompanied by a respect for the value of our own person, for each of us is a gift from eternity, as every other is a gift.

~

A caring response is sometimes not easy. A caring response is not a passive response. It means that whatever happens, we act in a way which shows our respect for each other and for our own selves. While a caring response is often not easy, it is possible, and it is the heart of a religious life.

When we do not live up to that standard as persons—and there will be times when we fail—then we must accept that we have fallen short. We must acknowledge that (at least to ourselves) and move on, not trapped by the past but open to new life. If we are ready and willing to be strong, we are ready to take on the world.

—

Rollo May said that anxiety is present in every authentic encounter *(Paulus).* There *is* a risk in meeting, an anxiety around being open to the new and in going forward to meet newness in our life situation and in people. We can be trapped by our need for security; we must have cycles in our lives of security and insecurity in order for us and our relationships to remain alive.

According to May, any continuing relationship—if it is to remain vital—must continue to have risk and anxiety within it. We constantly tend to make long-standing relationships (even close ones) become lifeless under a blanket of habitual responses and courtesies. Our relationships have a natural tendency to become reduced to a suffocating drama in which each person acts out a role frozen some time ago.

What are the risks of real meeting? What is there to be anxious about? There are many risks: the risk of being rejected by the other, and the risk that the other will *not* reject me, but will make himself or herself present to me, with his or her feelings and needs, values and concerns. Then I have to confront my own response or lack of response.

There are also these risks:
- that I may become aware of some aspect of myself in the relationship that I do not like;
- that I have to accept some responsibility for what happens in the relationship, and I may not want that responsibility;
- that I cannot control the relationship, since it depends upon the other person, and that other is free;
- that when my relationship with the other is opened up, it will result in a growing apart of the two of us and our separation.

These then are some of the risks of meeting. But if there are risks, there are even greater joys in accepting those risks and the anxieties that a full life demands. There is the joy of the earth-shaking experience of being accepted as we are with all our strengths and weaknesses, the joy of being confirmed as a human being. There is the joy when we become aware of noble feelings within ourselves, brought to the surface by the other person: feelings of compassion, of caring, of an accepting understanding, of the love called friendship and the love called agapé.

There is even a joy possible in becoming aware of feelings within us of which we are not proud and may be even ashamed, for the release of these dark aspects of ourselves brings relief, and gives an intensity to our lives as we come to terms with these dark aspects. Brought to light, they make clear the nature of our struggle to become larger, better persons. Our awareness of what we do not like in ourselves can lead us to accept ourselves with our strengths and weaknesses and to go on to confront those weaknesses.

In the risk of meeting we can know the joy of *not* having control, of being in a dance of life with another, in which each of us is free and at the same time part of something which transcends our solitary existence. Finally, when we have found a profound relationship with another in which we willingly risk all our risks, we can know the joy of growing together as we grow separately.

If we are to be truly alive, a leap of faith into the unknown is necessary, the kind of leap we must make all of our lives, time after time. Through our faith in life, which encourages us to make that jump into the unknown, we find life for ourselves, and become the instruments of life to others.

～

In our daily lives we become involved in the mundane, the habitual, the trifles which must be attended to. We see the face of another, but do not look at the other in his or her fullness of being. We hear another's words, but do not listen to the presence of the other beneath the words. May we have eyes to see, ears to hear, a heart to know, a mind to understand, and hands and voice to respond, so that we may live in the world with the full presence of our being.

～

We must be realistic about what is involved in an intimate relationship. Every close relationship will involve frustrations: we are not only going to be frustrated in attaining our realistic goals, but also in attaining our unrealistic goals. The process of coming to terms with our own unrealistic expectations of the other is a continuing one throughout that relationship, because the individuals themselves change over time and pass through different periods of life, which reveal new strengths and weaknesses. We discover and reveal different things about ourselves and others, and each new challenge requires something new of us.

～

If I bask in feelings of moral or intellectual superiority, if
I feel "holier than thou" or "smarter than thou", then I have
poisoned my capacity for compassion and understanding.
I will have also poisoned my ability to raise others'
consciousness and to persuade.

~

The message in *Gift From the Sea* by Anne Morrow Lindbergh
is that our relationships with nature and with one another—even
with those closest to us—are bound to be intermittent. If we are
relating to another as whole person to whole person, then there
will be times when that relationship will ebb and times when it
will flow.

Many relationships do not survive that ebb and flow. There are
those, says Lindbergh, who insist "on permanency, duration,
continuity, when the only continuity possible, in life as in love, is
in growth, in fluidity—in freedom, in the sense that the dancers
are free, barely touching as they pass, but partners in the same
pattern." Within a relationship (including the most intimate one
we have), there must be a natural ebb and flow, and the security of
that relationship depends upon our being able to accept it as it is
each moment.

Lindbergh speaks of the "security of the wingèd life." Indeed,
the security in our lives lies in our understanding and accepting the
ebb and flow of our relationships, so that we can live each moment
of ebb and flow. Beyond that, our ultimate security and our freedom lie in understanding that our life itself is intermittent: not
only are we touched by the tide, but we are ourselves part of a tide
that rises and falls on other human islands, and after we have
touched those islands, we roll at last to other, further shores.

~

In our silences may we feel one another's presence, and in the words with which we speak to one another, may we listen to hear the message that is beneath the words. In our efforts to bring justice to others, let us be concerned not only to do the right thing, but also to do the caring thing. So may we heal one another, rather than triumph over one another, and transform the lives of others and ourselves in a true victory of the spirit.

＿

One of the conditions for real intimacy is that we must be willing to regard the other person as he or she really is. Another condition—just as important—is that we must be willing to regard ourselves as we really are. We cannot be truly intimate with someone whom we are trying to impress, to whom we are trying to appear to be a certain kind of person. We can be intimate only with someone with whom we are willing simply to be ourselves.

We each decide upon the distance between ourselves and others, and we each decide when and whether we shall be open to the possibility of intimacy. We are under no heavenly compulsion to like everyone. If intimacy requires that we be honest with our own feelings, we cannot compel our feelings of indifference or dislike into their opposites. Kindness, consideration, and courtesy are universal virtues to exercise in our contact with every human being, but openness to intimacy is a matter for personal decision.

＿

We wish to live lives of goodness and compassion, but we are timid or insensitive to the particular occasions when we have the opportunity to live goodness. Too often we seek principles to justify our sloth or evasion of responsibility, and we pass by on the other side from those in need. May we come to know the meaning of caring, not in a sentimental effusion which comes and goes without lasting effect upon us or anyone else, but caring as good-will at work in partnership with reason. So may we transform ourselves and those around us.

―

Love is, as Martin Buber said, our capacity to see that we are intimately related to everyone else. We have the power, each of us, to confirm one another, not by protestations of love or sentimental declarations, but by the glance and the quiet word that affirm and by the caring act that needs no words to trumpet itself.

―

In our maturity we are most alive when we seek not to defend some idol of perfection we would like to think we are, but to know and to feel the ties that bind us to one another, imperfect though we may each be.

―

The ultimate ethical question is not "What is the right thing to do?" The question is rather "What is the caring thing to do? What is the loving thing to do? What is the loving thing to do for you and for me and for the others?" That is the religious question you and I face every day in a new form. That is the question that demands that we enlarge our souls if we wish to answer it.

―

a passion for justice

Injustice ultimately is not converted into justice by governmental or social agencies. Those agencies are simply weapons against injustice. Injustice is converted to justice only by the passion for justice of our own people, of ourselves.

～

As the world struggles to find a way to move from the anxiety of war, as we are reminded daily of millions who live in poverty or oppression, we are tempted to withdraw and to close our ears and our eyes to the troubling sights and sounds. We have sought the solace of religion without works, and peace without striving for peace; we have sought shelter from reality, rather than the courage to live in the real world. When we have done these things, we have only moved further away from the spirit of truth and the light which can illuminate our lives.

Let us turn from those who assure us with smooth words of comfort and conformity; may we ourselves be not spectators in the crowd, but instruments of the holy call for justice, truth, and love in action.

～

"Things" are in the saddle and ride us, said Thoreau. These "things" include not only material objects and desires, but also our subservience to our politics, our nationalism, our own ideas, and our own convictions of what is just or unjust.

If we take the time to cultivate our spiritual roots and to keep in touch with those roots, we shall get the things and opinions and ideologies out of the saddle. There is a nobility present in our nature as human beings, but we must cultivate that nobility. We see it shine in the faces and the works of the great souls of our time, but it can shine in each of us too if we let it, and it will light up our lives and the lives of those we love.

When we live spiritual lives, we shall come to live in a world we can enjoy. We shall come to deal with others (even those with whom we disagree) in the only way that will ever be able to persuade them: by appealing to the values and dreams that we have in common rather than by raising up the fears that separate us. We shall come to respond to human need out of our compassion, rather than from some cold calculus of benefits or from a political belief or ideology or a sense of national self-interest.

That is our dream, but it is a dream many are making real today, and it is a dream we can all make real tomorrow—we can live in the spirit of truth and love rather than the words of truth and love.

Let us seek to keep our minds free from the bondages of habit, class, and the comfort of too easy a conscience. May we listen to the voice of prophecy within each of us which allows us to judge not by the name of goodness, but by the true nature of goodness, to know what is good and what is evil.

May our impatience, disappointments, disgust, and sadness with the world not cause us to turn away from that world into apathy or cynical self-serving. Rather, let us be stirred by our conscience and the voice of prophecy within ourselves to turn to make our world a better, more beautiful, more honest, more caring place.

Let our individual acts be joined with those of all others of good will, so that our land is purged of its ugliness, its uncaring, its suffering, and its evils. So may we realize the faith which brought our country into being; so may we be worthy to bear the name "American."

～

The greatest threats to truth, justice, and caring come not from the obvious forces of falsehood and injustice, but from those institutions and persons who claim to speak and act in the name of virtue. We must demand from our institutions and leaders that they truly act on behalf of those they would serve.

May we demand from ourselves a courage to stand against the conventional wisdom and truth when we know in our hearts the conventions of our society are acting to hurt, to deny, or to ignore human need. So may we be worthy of the spirit which animates us to serve love, truth, and justice.

～

Our task is to use the common sense and moral values we believe in to confront death, disease, corruption, injustice, and evil. We are tough enough to face the real world. Ours does not have to be a religion of hothouse flowers.

If you expect human society to be moral and caring, you will break your heart. If you expect yourself to be morally perfect in this immoral society of ours, again, you will break your heart or the hearts of those who love you. But if you are willing to do some bit for the sake of justice in an unjust society, if you are willing to sacrifice concern for yourself because of your concern for others, then you will save your life in losing it.

If we cannot be saints, then our task is to keep the passion for justice and the love of life burning within ourselves, leaving aside the temptations of despair, or cynicism, or running away. Our task is to choose life over death in life!

~

In our daily lives we are beset by the cares and distractions of the everyday. We have in our search for comfort and respite often turned from the truth that speaks to us from the wretched of the earth, from those who suffer injustices, from those whose lives are blighted by each day. We evade, we rationalize, we seek the easy response, we harden our hearts.

May we find the courage to open our hearts to the cries of need and to understand that unless we listen to the uneasy voice of our conscience and respond to that voice, we add to the forces of human oppression and kill part of the life of our own souls.

~

In the service of freedom and liberty and of peace and justice, let us sacrifice our pride, our mean self-interest, our anger and hatred, our narrowness of interest, our lack of compassion for those not like us.

~

Seek what is most real, with passion, without the distractions of the mundane. May we rekindle our passion to seek the just— without becoming a victim of our own passion for justice—and rededicate ourselves to realize the best we can be and do, from this moment onward, without becoming absorbed in our own selves in our religious quest. Let us live in a love that seeks not its own, but is open to life in its fullest, and so know the freedom that comes to us in that love and that trust of life.

～

We are painfully aware that the hopes of the world for peace have not been realized; we have not been spared the scourge of war. We see human rights repressed throughout the world, the dignity of men and women and nations scorned; we see continuing poverty, intolerance, instability, and economic and military oppression.

May we have the courage to lift our eyes from our own feet to look those evils in the face; may we not seek escape in cries of futility nor in the false comfort of reliance on our political leaders to do those things we ourselves ought to do.

Let us be impelled by a vision of peace and dignity for all, a vision in which we maintain our hunger for peace and our thirst for righteousness, so that we each, in ways large or small, help to bring that vision into being. Remember that peace and righteousness come only to those who yearn for it, who work for it, and who sacrifice for it.

～

May we be part of the conscience of our nation and seek to arouse that conscience when our own consciences are aroused. Let us be alert to occasions when (as it was for the founders of our country) the legal violation of human rights and the legal infliction of injustice calls us to confront the legal process in the name of justice. When laws and customs impede, may we seek to modify those laws and customs to become more humane, ever mindful that our remedies do not create even greater evils than those we address.

So may we be true heirs of our heritage, in which eternal vigilance is the price of liberty. In all things let us act in hope and love and not in despair or rancor, so that we and our children continue to live in a land where justice and mercy depend ultimately not upon law, but upon the deeper source of justice and mercy in the hearts of our fellow citizens.

~

We struggle to uphold our deeply felt faith in the value of human life, but many of us differ from one another as to what serves life and what cheapens our reverence for life. Just as we oppose the imposition of others' beliefs upon us, may our passion for justice and truth not lead us to impose our beliefs or our judgments harshly on those who differ from us in good will, for it is only in our charity that we shall practice our faith and persuade, rather than offend. It is better to be compassionate and caring than to be right, it is better to be loving than to be judging, and if we all act in love, then ultimately we shall be just.

~

We fear to recognize the presence of injustice, because it calls upon us to join the struggle to set wrong right. We fear the truth about ourselves, because it may demand repentance and change. We resist those who bring us messages of justice denied and truth evaded. We resent victims of injustice and untruth because they trouble our sleeping consciences.

Let us seek the unease of truth and justice, rather than the comfort of ignorance. May we be part of the healing rather than the hurting in our world, and may we begin with our own eyes opened and our own consciences stirred. If we cannot do a great deal, let us each do a little, so that joined with others of good will, we move toward a world without needless suffering, hurt, hunger, and war.

～

We are oppressed by each day's report of injuries newly inflicted upon our fellow human beings by our fellow human beings. For the blighted lives of those who are violent and those who are victims of violence, we grieve. We grieve that the world dreamed for is not the world achieved. We are tempted to withdraw, to abandon hope that a day will come when violence, hatred, and war will be no more.

May we find courage to resist the temptation to retreat to a life of only self-service, and instead may we each in our own modest way do some work and support some effort to bring a healing to our troubled world. Let us begin with ourselves, using the power within each of us to leave the world a little better place for our having been here.

～

We struggle to be just and moral and caring. We are beset by the passionate cries of those who claim the universal truth or justice of their beliefs, and who would impose those beliefs upon those who see a different truth or who walk a different way. Let us not shrink before the clamor of the self-righteous, but struggle against our own sloth, fear, and comfort to enter the arena where the words of our compassion can be transformed into the reality of the acts of our caring.

～

We push forward, adventurers in living, moving to the last difficult frontiers where we must banish war, terror, poverty, and injustice. Let us remember how far we have come, and push on in our homes, our communities and wherever we may be, to the ultimate accomplishment of our human destiny: a world of peace and justice.

～

liberal religion: some beliefs

Religious liberals are united by a consensus on many beliefs.
We believe:

- in the sacredness of life;
- in the presence of moral character in each of us which gives us the power and the responsibility to make moral decisions and judgments for ourselves;
- that though we have an inexhaustible capacity for self-deception, we each also have a deeper ability to confront ourselves in our deceptions and to open them to the light of reasoned compassion, if we will to do so;
- that though evil often prospers, there is a power for good in each of us which we can bring forth so that our lives become instruments of good rather than evil;
- that although we are finite creatures subject to all the ills, the limitations, and the mortality of all life, we have

nevertheless within ourselves the power to bear those
limitations, endure suffering, and accept our mortality
with a courage and good will that makes our short span
of years worth its run.

Those are some of our basic beliefs. With all our beliefs (whatever
they may be for each of us), we know that we must be challenged
and confronted in those beliefs by the real and concrete issues of
daily life and our world. We remember that we too are subject to
our own idolatries and prejudices, and though we may be religious
liberals, we can be inhumane, inconsiderate, and self-serving in the
name of goodness or reason or science.

This is not a religious society of the elect in a world of lost
souls, nor is it a community of the saved in a world of the
damned. This is not an island of the pure in heart in a sea of the
impure, nor of saints among sinners. This is not a group of
rationalists in an ocean of superstition, nor of those who are free
of self-deception among a multitude of hypocrites.

Each of us from time to time is saved and lost in this world;
each of us is pure and defiled, rational and irrational, self-serving
and selfless, cruel and compassionate. We seek to remember who
we are, when we are saint and when we are sinner; we must
decide, each for himself or herself, what our religious and moral
way will be. We seek to be surprised: to rejoice when we are on
the right road, and to turn when we stray.

～

We are part of something that is real, that has meaning and
ultimate value. We believe in this reality whether or not we use
the word *God.* The most important principle of our beliefs is our
ultimate affirmation of existence, an affirmation not only of our
own personal existence, but of the entire cosmic creation of which
we are part. We see a shadow but still say our great *yes* in the face
of all that is good and all that is evil. It is in our ultimate

affirmation that we transform our own lives and become partners in creation, by joining our lives to the larger life that sent us forth and will gather us back. Ours is not an optimism that naïvely believes that all things turn out for the best, but an optimism that says *yes,* knowing all that we know and responding with a full heart.

⌇

Here are some of the articles of faith which many religious liberals share. We have faith:

- in the pursuit of truth, wherever it may lead us, uncomfortable though it may make us;
- in the goodness in most human beings, so that despite the rejections and disappointments we have had and will have, we shall risk reaching out again and again;
- that it is worthwhile for each one of us to do an act which helps heal a sick world, even if the magnitude of the problem lies beyond our small capacity to cure;
- in the power of love and of forgiveness, including the forgiveness of ourselves, and faith in the value of each human self, including ourselves, and in acting in ways which show care for each self, including our own selves;
- that life is worth living, though we are born to die from the moment we are conceived;
- that somehow we are more collectively than we are separately, and that we are enlarged by being together;
- that we shall pass through the valley of the shadow of destruction, and that one day true peace will come to our world.

⌇

What we need for a faith is not something to hate or to fear, but something to love and to trust. What most of us need is to be inspired by the life we live, to be filled with a spirit of life which gets us out of bed in the morning and about our business of making the lives of the people in the world close to us and distant from us better for our having got out of bed that morning. We need to be inspired to use whatever we have left of our own life as a gift of something precious which will never be repeated.

We believe that our lives must be lived in the presence of whatever is true, and we shall live in the light of that truth, even if it tells us that each of us is a terminal case and that our race is infinitesimal in the size and history of the universe which is our home.

We have a faith that we must look at the truth of the suffering world. We do not want to look at the suffering world, and we know that we do not have to look at the suffering world. There are many ways we can divert our eyes, but we believe that we must look, and when we look, respond. We are aware of our limitations in making as full a response as we can, but despite our evasions and procrastinations we turn back again and again to look at the suffering world and to respond to it. That reality commands us.

We have faith in the reality of this present moment. All the past and all the future is contained in this present moment, the only moment in which we live. We do not believe that the world we know in this moment is unreal, or that this moment is only a time of preparation for some future heavenly moment. We know that the only eternity we have is the one we already have: this present moment and each present moment. This present moment of reality commands us.

There are many other parts of our faith, and we vary with one another as to the contents of our personal faiths. With our faith we trust, or rather we entrust, our lives, and when we do that, our faith transforms us to see the world in a way we have not seen it before, in all its beauty and ugliness. It transforms us to act and to participate in what our faith tells us we must do, and it leads us to become co-creators ourselves. Commanded by our liberal faith, transformed by our participation in it, we are sustained by it.

We live in a time which demands of us that we commit ourselves to faith. Many religions have the power to transform the lives of their adherents (who experience life in vital ways they had not known before), and we too have a religion which can transform us in ways which honor our liberal faith and our personal freedom, a religion which can command, transform, and sustain us.

Only you can clarify your own faith; only you can commit yourself to it. There is a community of faith in which you can find and nurture that faith, in a world which cries out for your faith.

⮜

This shared faith of ours is not a creed that each of us must accept or repeat in order to be welcome among us. It is instead an expression of the spirit that brings us together and holds us together. Whether Christian, theist, or humanist, we believe that any faith or any ethics must be judged by its effects upon us personally, upon others, and upon the world we live in. If a faith hurts or destroys or diminishes, if it poses barriers to reconciliation and understanding, if it increases our fear, our hatred, and our treatment of others as less than fully human, then that faith is defective. We believe that whatever our beliefs, they must be humane in their effects, or they are unworthy of us and our responsibilities.

We share the belief that our religion and our ethics must be in accord with our best understanding of truth, as that truth is revealed to us by our reason and by science. We believe that every faith and every ethic at last resort cannot be proven like a geometric theorem, but requires the courage of a personal appeal to our intuition of truth. We believe that one test of that truth is that it violates neither science nor reason. Rationality and accord with science do not prove the truth of beliefs, but irrational and anti-scientific beliefs must be false.

We believe that each of us is the final arbiter for himself or herself as to what that personal faith should be. No clergy, no tradition, no authority is superior to our own judgment; but we believe that we must challenge our own judgment, testing it always against our temptations to self-deception and our prejudices of class, race, circumstance, and history. We are liable to faults of judgment and prejudice, but the remedy to those faults is our constant vigilance and resolve to be honest with our deepest selves.

We believe that each of us (except for a few who may be suffering profound defects of character or mental health) has access to a religious ground on which to stand. We may disagree whether that access is through the Christian or Jewish or some other tradition, or through opening ourselves to the experience of something transcendent and outside us, or through looking within ourselves, or through all of these sources. But we agree that each of us has access to the experience of being *at home* in the world and with our own selves.

Though we may differ in our faiths, we can reach out to one another when we are bruised and hurt, and even when we may not have the power to heal the wounds and restore the losses of others, we can help make those wounds and losses bearable. We show our true faith by our works, and what we do or leave undone tells more about what we believe than any creed or statement of belief.

We believe that we are more when we are in a community of seekers and believers than we are separately. In religious community and worship we can challenge one another in our self-deceptions, deepen our personal faith, elevate our moral aspirations, heighten our joy, and sustain one another in our sorrow.

By our faith, by our faiths, we shall live, bear our mortality, honor the human beings who have given us our existence, and leave the world a little better place than we found it.

⌇

The experience of the religious (that is, the experience of the spiritual quality of our lives) must be an individual experience. No group or congregation can be religious for us. But even so, our presence and participation in a congregation or religious group focuses our attention, through worship and our communal search, on a common element in our lives. In our sharing of personal experience we intensify our awareness of that experience and make ourselves more open to it. We come to realize that we are not solitary pilgrims, but a company of pilgrims, despite our varied theologies—Christian and non-Christian, theistic and non-theistic, traditional and non-traditional. We can pursue and find the religious in solitude, but we are more likely to find food for the soul if we attend a regular event with a spiritual menu.

⌇

We come to a religious community, one by one, in our solitary quest for a life of the spirit. We come to kindle the spirit that has died in us and to strengthen its flame when it is weak. We seek to be renewed from the banality and the shallowness of our lives; with consciences numbed and weakened by a world of suffering, destruction, and moral laziness, we come to have our consciences stirred again.

We seek to minister to one another by our common presence, for we have felt the strength that arises from the joining together of kindred seekers, a strength that comes to us that we might never know in our solitary pilgrimage.

We come not simply to be renewed by our sense of community in our common quest, but to find within our participation together the reawakening of our awareness that our own lives are part of a larger life; that through each of us the Universe becomes conscious of itself; that through each of us the spirit of truth and caring is brought to birth again and again, by what we learn, by what we feel, by the stirring within our souls of a caring love, and by what we do to be the living and acting conscience of the Universe.

I do not believe it is possible to live as an agnostic, as someone who throws up his or her hands and says, "I don't know—it's all too uncertain." We must each of us live by some kind of a faith. It may be a tentative faith, subject to change by tomorrow's experience or discovery, but it is a faith. It may be a faith in something unworthy—like faith in the ultimate value of property—or it may be an evil faith, like that of Jim Jones' cult. But if we are to live in an awareness that each of our lives will have its grief and trouble, and that we shall each of us one day be dead, then we either live by some faith in something that lives beyond us or we shut out an important and most human part of our consciousness.

My faith is simple: I believe that I live in a universe completely indifferent to my existence, indifferent to my joy and my sorrow. I was given life by my parents and the life force in the world that was expressed through them. When I die, I may be mourned by a few while their lives and memories last, but then all that was of me will be gone.

I do not seek consolation in a vision of some survival beyond the grave. The love and acceptance by my family and friends have given me as much as I desire from life. I have been schooled by many religions and by poets, artists, and composers. I have learned from them that in my minor life I have been part of one life that began with the birth of time and which will last as long as time lasts. I have been a small co-creator with the source of all Creation, and that is glory enough. My task is to develop the best that is in me and to use whatever powers and gifts I may have in service and celebration of life.

Simply letting the universe be what it is, without any name, in all its power, beauty, terror, and indifference, I am then neither a theist nor a non-theist. Yet, I do have faith that each of us, if we open ourselves to realize that we are an intimate part of one great whole—if we give up our attachment to ourselves—that each of us can receive what Christians call grace. The gift of life includes the gift of the power to prevail over everything that we encounter, if we open ourselves to receive that gift.

As I get older, I realize more and more the fullness of each moment as it comes. Nothing more than that is needed. This is my odyssey; this is my faith. Now it is time for me to go again, and I leave you with a poem translated from the Chinese:

> Over our cups of wine, in the arbor by the stream
> We talked and talked until, it seemed,
> We left no subject in all the world, from east to west,
>   untouched.
> And now my cart has rumbled off
> And when I turn my head to see you once again
> You are lost from sight, old friend,
> Hidden by the autumn rain.

There is nothing I can give you which you do not have
But there is much that, while I cannot give it,
You can take.

No heaven can come to us
Unless our hearts find rest in today.
Take heaven.

No peace lies in the future
Which is not hidden in this present moment.
Take peace.

The gloom of this world is but a shadow;
Behind it yet within reach is joy; there is radiance and glory
In the darkness could we but see, and to see
We have only to look. I beseech you to look.

Life is so generous a giver, but we, judging its gifts by their covering,
Cast them away as ugly or heavy or hard.
Remove the covering, and you will find beneath it
A living splendor, woven of love, by wisdom, with power.

Welcome it, grasp it, and you touch the angel's hand
That brings it to you. Everything we call a trial, a sorrow or a duty;
The angel's hand is there; the gift is there, and the wonder of an
Overshadowing presence.
Our joys too, be not content with them as joys.
They too conceal diviner gifts.

And so at this time I greet you: not quite as the world
Sends greetings, but with profound esteem
And the prayer that for you, now and forever,
The day breaks and shadows fall away.

-Fra Giovanni (16th c.), *Christmas Greeting*
(frequently quoted by Senghas)

notes

notes

notes